Charles Daly

The settlement of the Jews in North America

Charles Daly

The settlement of the Jews in North America

ISBN/EAN: 9783337136031

Printed in Europe, USA, Canada, Australia, Japan

Cover: Foto ©ninafisch / pixelio.de

More available books at **www.hansebooks.com**

THE Settlement of the Jews

IN NORTH AMERICA.

BY

CHARLES P. DALY, LL.D.
President of the American Geographical Society,

EDITED, WITH NOTES AND APPENDICES, BY

MAX J. KOHLER, A.M., LL.B.

NEW YORK:
PHILIP COWEN, 213-215 EAST 44TH STREET.
1893.

PREFACE.

More than twenty years have now elapsed since Judge Daly's work was first presented to the public, yet I feel that no excuse or apology is necessary for its re-publication to-day.

Mr. Daly, then Chief Justice of the Court of Common Pleas of this city, originally prepared the work in the form of an address delivered at the celebration of the 50th anniversary of the Hebrew Benevolent Society of New York, on April 11, 1872, and then enlarged it for publication in *The Jewish Times* of that year. Subsequently, the accomplished and erudite author utilized a portion of the same data in an address delivered at the laying of the corner-stone of the new Hebrew Orphan Asylum, New York, May 17, 1883.* It seems to me that the work has not lost the smallest element of interest since that time, but, on the contrary, appeals to-day to a much larger public than then, and, as, unfortunately, it did not appear in durable form, will seem to be new to the large majority of its readers of to-day. Here and there, the student of American Jewish history has, since its original appearance, re-discovered Judge Daly's work in out-of-the-way and few-and-far-between corners, and drawn upon it as by far the

---

* This address was printed in full in THE AMERICAN HEBREW at the time and published in pamphlet form.

most valuable, comprehensive and interesting work on the subject. Many others, to my knowledge, have, after search, been unable to obtain the work, and the purpose of the present re-publication is to make it accessible to these, as well as to the large public whom the work will please for more general reasons. The causes of our interest in a work like the present are numerous and varied. Perhaps the most natural source of interest is our race pride, our gratification over the deeds of members of our race, present or past, purely because of our common ties of race.

Often this interest in and enthusiasm over our past is not only justifiable but commendable. When a recent emigré, like Goldwin Smith, has the arrogance and effrontery to characterize the Jews, especially those of America, as parasites, who wait till others have sown and then rush in to divide with them the harvest, it is well to point to co-religionists who for centuries were engaged in this country in the arduous, and often unproductive occupation of sowing, as a conclusive refutation of such assertions, born of ignorance and prejudice. In this sense we may be proud and rejoice that Jews were interested co-workers in the discovery, settlement and development of our land, and acquaint ourselves as well as our Christian neighbors with those incidents in our national history.

The work under consideration appeals to us also in other ways. No statement has, perhaps, come to be better recognized than that we cannot understand the present without a study of the past. Incidents and traits suddenly come to the surface which a necessarily superficial consideration of present conditions does not explain. Other forces besides those we generally recognize, are working about us, and not the less effectively because the shallow, practical man of to day fails to note them. Problems of the present may often be solved by a study of past experiences. Besides, it has at length become recognized here and abroad that American Judaism has its own peculiar characteristics, virtues and vices, its own line of development. A work like the present one throws much new light and adds considerable interesting data to a study of these questions.

Since Judge Daly's work first appeared, there has been a sweeping revolution apparent in American Judaism. He wrote about the middle of the German-Jewish migration to America; since then other and far more numerous classes of Jews have arrived here, while their predecessors have multiplied and thrived. Our charities have increased and developed beyond all expectations, our standing and influence in the community even more so. But what interests us even more at this point is the intellectual development of the body of American Jews. We have erected and patronize scores of libraries. We have representatives in the faculties of nearly all our large colleges, many distinguished scholars among them. The Jewish press has increased in influence as well as numerically. Jewish Publication Societies which failed to interest enough persons then, are to-day in that respect at least, thriving. Is it not time, then, that we take more interest in our past, and proceed to study it more carefully, and not content ourselves with stopping at a period two thousand years behind us? Perhaps the best answer to the question is the establishment of the American Jewish Historical Society, with many able workers enlisted in its service. The formation of such a society and the promises it offers for the future, seem to me the best proofs possible that the publication to day of Judge Daly's work, will not be followed by twenty years of inactivity and lack of interest in continuing and developing the subject-matter. No better work to start with, upon which to build, than Judge Daly's can be conceived of. Almost every line affords a chance for interesting elaboration and investigation. Nor can anything more conducive to systematic study and intelligent collection of data be obtained. Even at the last meeting of the Historical Society, there were several clear cases of unconscious re-discovering of data known to and employed by Judge Daly. It is with the expectation that the republication of the present work will be of interest and profit to the general public, as well as to the scholar, that it appears anew to-day. It is not for me to praise Judge Daly's work; the reader will soon have an opportunity to do that himself. I may be pardoned, however, if I add that the narrative is always interesting, no matter how trivial the incident might appear, if elaborated by some less able pen. Besides the most intimate acquaintance with the data of New York and American history generally, Judge Daly's work is characterized by absolute accuracy of statement and impartiality of treatment. It is therefore with pleasure that we turn to his account of a people whom he describes as having "dwelt upon this island for more than two centuries, and who, though not, until a recent period, very numerous, have, as an integral portion of our population, exercised a very material influence upon the commercial development and prosperity of this city."

Judge Daly's work, as it originally appeared, contained numerous citations of authorities in the footnotes. The editor has materially increased these, so as to render the work more valuable to the student, has verified almost every statement, and added some additional notes bearing on the text. All his notes are signed "Editor." He has also supplied an Introduction, based largely on a paper read by him before the American Jewish Historical Society in Philadelphia in December, 1892, upon "The Beginnings of New York Jewish History." He also wishes to add that he has attempted throughout to preserve absolutely the identity of Judge Daly's work, and has therefore in several instances reluctantly omitted notes bearing only distantly on the text.

His thanks are due to Judge Daly for kindly consenting to the republication of the work. Furthermore, Judge Daly kindly volunteered to write an additional instalment for this series; it is needless to say that his offer has been gratefully accepted. This new portion will appear as a supplementary instalment.

MAX J. KOHLER.

INTRODUCTION.

About 70 years ago an astute Yankee, after having traveled about abroad for some time, wrote a book in which he described, among the other things which had come under his observation, the unfortunate condition of the Jews in Europe, especially of Italy. He expresses surprise that the Jews had not availed themselves of America's civil and religious liberty, and accounts for the fact in two ways: "The one theory is based on their reputed dread of the sea, 'for the water,' say they, 'hath no beams.' Another reason is predicated on the proverbial astuteness of us New Englanders, with whom not even the Jews dare venture into competition." If our Yankee were to reappear in our midst to-day, I think he would be bound to confess either that human nature had changed since his day, or that neither of his two theories is satisfactory. I have availed myself of his amusing statement, however, because it is a capital illustration of the popular ignorance of American-Jewish history which has not yet disappeared, even mong the American Jews themselves as a body. While Judge Daly's work is the most interesting and important presentation of the claims of the Jews to credit for long association with the destinies of our country from early colonial times down to our own day, the last few years have opened up a field of research which gives promises of rich returns, going to show that the Jews have been actively interested in the discovery, colonization and settlement of America from the days of Columbus on. I propose to dwell on this subject in this brief Introduction to Judge Daly's work.

Prof. M. Kayserling has made the department of Spanish-Jewish relations to the Discovery and Colonization of the New World peculiarly his own. While his early works on "Sephardim" and "Portuguese Discoveries" only touched on America, his recent investigations—so far as we can judge from his interesting article on "The First Jew on American Soil" in *The Menorah* for October, 1892, and the reports received from him and not yet published, based on personal examination of the Spanish archives with particular view to this subject—will be authoritative expositions of the work of the Jews in this connection. Nor is it strange that the Jews should have actively participated in the work of Spanish and Portuguese explorers. The indebtedness of the modern world to the brilliant achievements of the Moors in the way of navigation and geographical science, which alone made the era of discoveries possible, is to-day recognized. Yet the direct connection of the Moors with Christian Europe was infinitesimal. As in the case of medicine and in the various industries, so also here, the Jews became the intermediaries between Moors and Christians, and imparted the scientific discoveries which the former so liberally shared with them, and which they themselves did something towards enlarging, to Christian Europe, during and after the Moorish occupation of Spain. Various writers have touched on this subject from time to time, and it is indeed an interesting one. I may be pardoned, however, for calling attention to a valuable paper, collecting much of the data on the subject by my father, Rev. Dr. K. Kohler, read before the German Historical Society of New York, and printed in the *Belletristisches Journal* in May, 1891; a rather inadequate translation of the same, printed without the author's supervision, appeared in *The Menorah* for July, 1891.

Eugene Lawrence, in a valuable article on "The Mystery of Columbus," which appeared in *Harpers' Monthly* recently (April, 1892), indicates briefly the work of the Jews in this direction. Their work may be briefly summarized as having been: first, in spreading and developing geographical science; next, in participating in some of the colonizing expeditions themselves, though under serious difficulties and under disguised names and professions of religion; and, lastly, in some of the early settlements themselves. Prof. Kayserling has proven that there were secret Jews (Maranos) with Columbus on his first voyages, one of whom at once settled in Cuba, and that there were Jewish financiers who aided Columbus in securing the funds for his voyages. Because of royal interdictions and fears of the Inquisition, it is extremely difficult to identify the Jews in these expeditions. The same is true of the early settlements in America under the Spanish and the Portuguese, as in Mexico and Brazil. In the former country, scarcely any but those whom the Inquisition, unfortunately for them, exposed as Jews, can be to-day recognized. Of the latter, it seems clear that Jews settled in the country as early as 1548, living generally as New Christians. During the short-lived Dutch occupation of Brazil, they resumed their Jewish worship, but paid the penalty in part at least with their lives when the Portuguese regained control. But this portion of our history is still so fragmentary and obscure, that we cannot profitably linger over it, especially as it is rather foreign to our subject, the history of the Jews in North America.

There is one further departure from the subject, for which I must, however, ask the reader's kind indulgence, especially as I hope to show that the whole matter is intimately connected with the first arrival of Jews in New York. I shall proceed to set this forth at some length.

In 1859, a paper was read before the New York Historical Society by Rev. Dr. A. Fischell of New York, on The History of the Jews in America, which led to an interesting discussion in which the lecturer was forced to take sides against the American historian George Bancroft on the question whether the Jews had enjoyed fuller liberties in Rhode Island under Roger Williams' successors than under the Dutch, Bancroft espousing the cause of the former, Dr. Fischell of the latter. This is an interesting question because, while we are constantly reminded of Rhode Island's toleration, the Dutch do not generally receive due credit for this trait from American historians. As a large portion of Judge Daly's work is devoted to the history of the Jews in places settled by the Dutch, — for the Jewish settlement in New York gave rise to a number of others,— this subject of Dutch toleration is of considerable interest to us. This work will show that, neither under the Dutch nor in Rhode Island, were the rights of the Jewish settlers as extensive as those of the adherents of the prevailing religions. Nor does it appear that the Dutch government originally intended to pursue the same policy of religious toleration as to her colonial possessions as she adopted at home, for we know that the very Puritans who were permitted to enjoy Amsterdam's generous hospitality and toleration, were refused permission to settle in the Dutch Colonies, prior to arranging for the colony which was subsequently planted at Plymouth.

It required the leveling and humanizing influences of Commerce to bring about religious toleration, and this explains the fact that the Dutch West India Company took a different attitude in this matter than the Government, in sanctioning and encouraging the settlement of the Jews in New Netherland. The letter directed by the Dutch West India Company Directors to Stuyvesant, containing this grant, is interesting as showing the conflict between old-time prejudice and intolerance and the commercial instinct of the Dutch as to the desirability of giving the permission prayed for. The words "and also because of the large amount of capital which the Jews have invested in the shares of this Company," were no doubt a very important argument in favor of making the concession.

But it is my privilege to point out a much earlier connection between the Jews and the Dutch West India Company, which colonized New Netherland. It appears that William Usselinx, who had for many years agitated the question of incorporating the Company, but had not found a favorable ear till 1620 or thereabouts, was annoyed to find that the States General had received a draft of a proposed charter for a West India Company which differed in several essential features from the one he had proposed. The opposition charter provided for a series of attacks on the Spanish silver fleets by the Company's vessels and for means for depriving the Dutch of their Brazilian settlements. One of the chief arguments in favor of this proposition was the assistance that would be secured from the Jews who were settled in Brazil and who had offered to co-operate with the Dutch, so as to secure the more liberal Dutch rule instead of the harsh and intolerant Portuguese. In Dr. Jameson's[1] interesting biography of William of Usselinx,

---

[1] American Historical Association Papers, Vol. II. p. 76, and authorities cited there.

several letters from Usselinx to the States General are found, with references to other, original authorities, which bear out my statements.

In one of these letters we find Usselinx assailing this proposed charter by means of a most savage attack on the Jews: "No trust should be put in the promises made there (in Brazil) by the Jews, a race faithless and pusillanimous, enemies to all the world and especially to all Christians, caring not whose house burns, so long as they may warm themselves at the coals, who would rather see a hundred thousand Christians perish than suffer the loss of a hundred crowns." Usselinx's abuse was of no avail, however, for the modified charter was adopted despite his opposition, and the demand for shares in the Company, which had been rather lax before, was greatly increased. Nor is this surprising, for the trade between New Netherland and Holland in those days, especially when compared with the enormous amount of the Company's capital, was trifling indeed. It may well be claimed that the Company would have had a very brief and uneventful history, had it not been for the two features in question. I doubt whether the Dutch West India Company would ever have settled New York, and still more whether it would have been able to sustain the infant colony, had it not been for them. One year a dividend of 75 per cent was declared on the six million gulden capital, in consequence of the capture of the Spanish silver fleet. I have already cited the clause from an official letter showing that the Jews were heavily interested in the company's stock. I may add that Menasseh ben Israel in his "Humble Address to Cromwell," states that "the Jews were enjoying a good part of the (Dutch) East and West India Companies." Judge Daly is furthermore authority for the statement that the Company had several

Jewish directors. It seems to me to be a very reasonable supposition that Jews were among the projectors of the Company, for it could only have been to their own co-religionists that the Brazilian Jews would have communicated their proffers of aid in case of a Dutch attack on Brazil, for they were living in Brazil under the guise of New Christians, and would not have ventured to expose themselves to any but co-religionists.

Nor were the promises of aid on the part of the Brazilian Jews idle and untrustworthy, Usselinx to the contrary notwithstanding. In De Beauchamp's Histoire du Brêsil II p. 159 and in Southey's History of Brazil (Second edition I, pp. 477, 479, 495, supplemental note no. 135 and vol. II p. 241) we read that before the Dutch fleet directed against Brazil put to sea, the States General obtained most useful information as to the condition of affairs in Brazil through the intermediation of Jews who were settled there, and who nearly all ardently desired to become subjects of the United States because of their great toleration in religious matters.

Unfortunately for these Jews, the first Dutch occupation of Brazil was short-lived, and their fate when the Portuguese regained control was such as we have elsewhere stated. When the Dutch again came into power those that had escaped death again threw off the guise of Christians and lived avowedly as Jews, until by the terms of the first Dutch capitulation in 1654, the Portuguese again became the masters. By the express terms of the capitulation, the Portuguese promised the Jews "an amnesty, in all wherein they could promise it," words which left an ominous latitude for intolerance. That very year, a party of Jews left Bahia and took passage in the ship St. Catrina, which arrived soon after in New Amsterdam. It is with their history and that of their co-religionists who subsequently followed their example in settling in North America, that Judge Daly's work deals.

M. J. K.

The Settlement of the Jews in North America.

THE SETTLEMENT OF THE JEWS IN NORTH AMERICA.

When I consented to comply with the request made, that I would address the audience assembled here this evening, it occurred to me, that an occasion so interesting as the celebration of the fiftieth anniversary of the oldest benevolent institution established by people of the Jewish persuasion in the City of New York, would be an appropriate one, upon which to give some account of the first settlement of the Jewish people in this city, and of their early history. The facts, so far as I am aware, have never been collected and put in any narrative form. Our local or state histories contain very little upon the subject. Even our latest and fullest historian, Mr. Brodhead, mentions, I think, but two circumstances in connection with a people who have dwelt upon this island for more than two centuries, and who, though not, until a recent period, very numerous, have, as an integral portion of our population, exercised a very material influence upon the commercial development and prosperity of this city.

Having given much attention to our early annals, and having had occasion very frequently to consult the documents and records, which constitute the material, from which our municipal history is derived, I shall be enabled to put together with but little effort the information they supply of the first settlement of people of the Jewish faith in this city and of what is known respecting them here for at least the first century and a half. In commencing this inquiry, it may gratify those present to be able to state, and especially upon the semi-centennial of this benevolent institution, that one of the earliest documents, showing the existence here of people of the Jewish persuasion, is the record of an act of benevolence on the part of a Jew to a friendless Christian stranger, and certainly the history of no people in any place can begin with an incident more creditable to them than the exercise of that charity which is limited to no sect or creed— which recognizes but two things, the existence of want and the ability to relieve it.

It is no doubt known to many here, that this city was founded by the Dutch and that for the first half century of its existence it was in possession of and governed by people from Holland. The first Jewish emigration occurred during this period, and it may be of interest to give some account of the circumstances which led to it.

It occurs in the wise purpose of the Great Ruler of the Universe, that calamitous events are not infrequently accompanied by other events, which mitigate the force of the calamity and prevent its occurrence thereafter. No event has proved more beneficial to the Jewish people than the discovery of America, and yet the very year that it occurred was 1492, the year of the commencement of the terrible persecution of the Jews in Europe, which led to their expulsion from France, Spain and Portugal, an event in its immediate effects more disastrous to them than even the destruction of Jerusalem. Spain, the chief agent in that terrible work and the most intolerant and cruel of the nations of Europe, having, during her despotic rule afterwards in the Low Countries, undertaken to crush out there all freedom of opinion, encountered a spirit of resistance on the part of the brave descendants of those Batavian tribes that had rescued Holland from the sea, which culminated in that great political event in 1572, known as the

Revolt of the Netherlands. The famous union of Utrecht was followed by the noble declaration of William the Silent, upon being installed as Stadholder in 1581, that "he should not suffer any man to be called to account, molested or injured for his faith and conscience," and when by the Truce of Antwerp in 1609, the freedom of the Netherlands was assured, the Dutch signalized their independence by throwing open their country to the persecuted of all sects and nations. Among the earliest to avail themselves of this place of refuge were the Jews, and persons of that persuasion flocked in from Spain, Portugal, Germany and Poland, settling in the free cities of Holland and especially in the commercial city of Amsterdam. Amsterdam presented the spectacle of a city where all religions were tolerated, and where men of all shades of political opinion found themselves secure in their persons and property. By a writer of that day it was stigmatized as "a common harbor of all opinions and of all heresies." By another, in the figurative language then in fashion, "as a cage of unclean birds," and even Andrew Marvel, the friend of Milton and the incorruptible patriot, wrote a derisive poem upon Holland, in which Amsterdam was described with its mixed population of "Turk, Christian, Pagan, Jew," its "bank of conscience," where "all opinions found credit and exchange;" closing his poem with a line, which he certainly meant in no spirit of compliment:

"The universal church is only there."

Among the Jewish emigrants who then flocked into Holland, the most numerous and the most cultivated were the Jews from Portugal, many of them coming from Leira, a town in the province of Estramadura, which enjoys the honor of being the third place in

Europe in which a printing press was set up, the commercial progress and prosperity of which was due in a large measure to its highly intelligent and industrious Jewish population as its decline may be attributed to their expatriation and expulsion. The Portuguese Jews settled chiefly in Amsterdam, where they were distinguished by their industry, energy, intelligence and probity, and here at this period, 1632, the philosopher Spinoza, the child of two of these Jewish emigrants, was born.

The tolerant spirit of Holland found its fruits in the rapid advance of the Dutch in all commercial pursuits. A distinction was made in favor of the Reformed Protestant faith, which was by law the established religion, but all others were tolerated. Though the position of the Jews in Holland was in marked contrast with every other part of Europe, they were not entirely free from restrictions. They were by law forbidden to write or speak disparagingly of the Christian religion, or to make converts. They were not allowed to intermarry with Christians, nor to follow any mechanical pursuit, or to engage in retail trade, but were in all other respects admitted to full political privileges with the rest of their fellow-citizens.

They were at first required to exercise the rites of their religion within the privacy of their own houses, or at least in houses not having the outward appearance of religious edifices. This restriction was removed when Louis Napoleon, the brother of Napoleon I, became King of Holland; and when I was in Amsterdam twenty years ago, the Portuguese Synagogue there was regarded as one of the finest in Europe. It was certainly more imposing than the one I visited in Leghorn, then said to be the largest on the Continent; but both were interesting in my

eyes as early monuments of entire religious freedom.
The Jews of Amsterdam, through their capacity for
business, their energy and their integrity, became
wealthy and influential, and were shareholders to a
large amount in the West India Company, the commercial corporation by which the City of New York
was founded. This body, though ostensibly incorporated to promote the settlement of new countries and
for the general purpose of traffic, was in reality organized to secure pecuniary gain through the capture of
the richly laden Spanish vessels, and by the seizure
of the Spanish and Portuguese possessions in
the West Indies and South America. In fact, the
States General, as one of the means of crippling
Spain, acquiesced in the exercise by this corporation of
the warlike powers of a nation and it had at one time
no less than seventy armed vessels in its service. Its
object in founding New York was not the establishment of a city upon the banks of the Hudson, but to
have a haven for its vessels there in connection with
a more extended field of operations in the West Indies
and South America. In 1630 Bahia or St. Salvador,
then the capital of Brazil, was captured by its fleet
and from that time to 1642, its career was one of conquest in Brazil. Bahia was then, as it is still, a place
of great maritime importance, and when the West
India Company threw open the trade of Brazil in
1638, the Portuguese Jews of Amsterdam emigrated
to Bahia in considerable numbers, to which they
were attracted not only by the advantage of trade,
but as the capital of a country where they could speak
their native language, and under Dutch rule enjoy
entire freedom of religion. "They proved to be,"
says Southey,(1) "excellent colonists, exhibiting their

---

1. Southey, History of Brazil, Vol I p. 644.

characteristic industry." Upon the settlement in Bahia and other parts of Brazil, many Portuguese there, he says, threw off the mask and joined their co-religionists. "The open joy," he further observes, "with which they celebrated their religious rites and ceremonies attracted too much notice. The public exercise of their religion excited the horror of the Catholics, and as the Dutch Protestants united with the Catholics, the government was constrained to declare that the religious liberty allowed in Holland did not extend to Brazil, and an edict was passed requiring the Jews to perform their religious rites and services thereafter in private."

After 1642, the power of the Dutch in Brazil was gradually weakened. Its possession exhausted the resources of the West India Company, and as the government of Holland had made peace with Portugal and would not support the company in its efforts to retain their possession, they were compelled to withdraw their troops and evacuate the country. We find that the year when this took place, 1654, was the year of the first arrival of Jews in the city of New York, or, as it was then called New Amsterdam, and they came beyond any doubt from Bahia, abandoning Brazil when it was evacuated by their Dutch protectors. Twenty-seven persons, men, women and children, (2) arrived here in the autumn of 1654, in the barque St. Catarina, of which Jacques de la Motthe was master, from Cape St. Anthony, or as the Portuguese call it, San Antonio; Cape St . Anthony being the projection of land which forms one side of the Bay of Bahia and occupies the space between the city and the ocean. Their departure appears to have been sudden, for upon their arrival here, their goods

---

2. V. M. 1849 p. 383. Ed. 1860, p. 615.

were sold by the master of the vessel at public auction for the payment of their passage and the amount realized by the sale being insufficient, he applied to the Court of Burgomaster and Schepens for an order that one or two of them, as principals, be held as security for the payment of the balance in accordance with the contract made with him by which each person signing it had bound himself for the payment of the whole amount, and under which he had taken two of them, David Israel and Moses Ambrosius, as principal debtors. The Court accordingly ordered that they should be placed under civil arrest, in the custody of the provost marshal until they should have made satisfaction, that the captain should be answerable for their support whilst in custody, as security for which a certain proportion of the proceeds of the sale of the goods was directed to be left in the hands of the Secretary of the colony (3), but as no fur-

---

3. The official account of the matter reads as follows:
"Extraordinary Meeting, holden on
  Wednesday, the 16th September, 1654,
Present,   At the City Hall,
  The Heeren,
    Arent Van Halten,
    M. Krigier,
    Pieter Wolfertsen,
    Oloff Stevenson and
    Cornelis Van Tienhoven.
Jacques de la Motthe, master of the Bark called St. Catrina, Plaintiff
  contra
David Israel and the other Jews, according to their signatures, Defts.
  Touching the ballance of the payment of the passage of the said Jews, for which each is bound *in Solidum*. Whereas, their goods sold thus far by vendue, do not amount to the payment of their obligation, it is, therefore, requested that one or two of the said Jews be taken as principle (principals??) which, according to the aforesaid contract or obligation, cannot be refused. Therefore he hath taken David Israel and Moses Ambrosius as principal debtors for the remaining ballance, with request that the same be placed in confinement until the account be paid.

ther proceedings appear upon the records, the matter was doubtless arranged and was probably nothing more than a dispute or misunderstanding between them and the captain as to whether they were bound to make good the deficiency, which was probably enhanced by the forced sale of their effects at auction. From these proceedings I infer that they left Brazil hastily, taking with them what effects they could, the evacuation of the country by the Dutch leaving them without protection, and the apprehension of persecution leading them to seize the earliest opportunity to get within the friendly shelter of a Dutch colony. This event is one of interest, as it was in all probability the first arrival of people of the Jewish persuasion within the limits of what is now the United States (4)

Whatever may have been the disposition of the inhabitants to the newcomers, the feeling of the Governor, Stuyvesant, was hostile. He was a man of strong will and of strong prejudices, and shortly after their arrival, he wrote to the directors in Ams-

---

The Court having weighed the petition of the plaintiff, and seen the obligation wherein each is bound *in Solidum* for the full payment, have consented to the plaintiff's request, to place the aforesaid persons under civil arrest (namely with the Provost Marshal) until they shall have made satisfaction, provided, that he, La Motthe, shall previously answer for the board, which is fixed at 16 stivers per diem for each prisoner; and is ordered, that for this purpose 40—50 guilders, proceeding from the goods sold, shall remain in the hands of the Secretary, together with the expenses of this special court. Done in New Amsterdam in New Netherland." Valentine's Manual for 1849, page 383,—EDITOR.

4. This statement has been rendered rather doubtful, as it appears from a paper recently read before the American Jewish Historical Society by Mr. Jacob H. Hollander of Baltimore on "John Lumbrozo," that names that appear to be pronouncedly Jewish, are found in the Maryland Annals a number of years before this time.—EDITOR.

terdam, requesting that "none of the Jewish nation be permitted to infest New Netherland." The answer was worthy of Holland—that his request "was inconsistent with reason and justice." (5) In fact, the company were favorable to the emigration of Jews to their newly acquired possession in America. Not only, as I have said, were the Jews of Amsterdam large stockholders of the company, (6) but several of that persuasion were in the Board of Directors. In 1652, a tract of land of two leagues along the coast for every fifty families, and of four leagues for every hundred families, was granted in the island of Curacoa to Joseph Nunez de Fonseca, and others to found a colony of Jews in that island. Fonseca, who was afterwards a merchant in Curacoa, together with one Jan de Illan, who went out as a patroon, made the attempt, but it was not successful, there

---

5. The instructions to Stuyvesant from the Directors of the Company were to this effect, as contained in the official records:

"26th of April, 1655.

"We would have liked to agree to your wishes and request, that the new territories should not be further invaded by people of the Jewish race, for we foresee from such immigration the same difficulties which you fear, but after having further weighed and considered the matter, we observe that it would be unreasonable and unfair, especially because of the considerable loss sustained by the Jews in the taking of Brazil, and also because of the large amount of capital which they have invested in shares of this company. After many consultations we have decided and resolved upon a certain petition made by said Portuguse Jews, that they shall have permission to sail to and trade in New Netherland and to live and remain there, provided the poor among them shall not become a burden to the company, or to the community, but be supported by their own nation. You will govern yourself accordingly."—Documents Relating to the Colonial History of the State of New York. Vol. XIV, p. 315.—EDITOR.

6. See Introduction for further details as to this question.— EDITOR.

being not more than twelve settlers on the tract. (7) Stuyvesant's letter, therefore, instead of producing what he desired had a very opposite effect, for it stirred up the Jewish members of the Board of Directors to apply for distinct privileges for their coreligionists, and a special act was issued on the 15th of July, 1655, expressly permitting Jews to trade to New Netherland, and to reside there on the simple condition only, that they should support their own poor; (8) a condition, it may be said, which they have strictly fulfilled ever since, for few, if any, of their denomination have ever in this city been supported at the public charge.

Before the intelligence of this act could have reached New Netherland, an additional number of Jews arrived here directly from Holland, who probably came in anticipation of some such measure, or with the knowledge of the disposition of the company. (9) Their arrival and a circumstance that occurred about the same time, had an unfavorable effect upon Stuyvesant, and led him to adopt

---

7. See Calendar of Historical Manuscripts. Edited by E. B. O'Callaghan. Dutch Manuscripts. Curacoa Papers, pp. 329-330, also Correspondence, p. 289 —EDITOR.

8. I have been unable to find an order bearing this date; I believe that the one already given (in Note 5) is the one in question, for it clearly contains the condition that the Jews shall provide for their own poor.—EDITOR.

9. In a subsequent letter, dated June 14, 1656, and found in Note No. 11, and also in a petition by Abraham de Luceña and others referred to in the text and to be found in Note 17, "orders of Feb. 15th, 1655, issued at the request of the Jewish or Portuguese nation," are referred to. The official records extant do not contain any order of so early a date, but if, as seems likely to me, such orders were issued but have been lost since, the arrival of these Dutch Jews is easily accounted for, as being sanctioned by the company. Their arrival is referred to in the next note.— EDITOR.

energetic measures. On the 1st of March, 1655, one Abraham De La Simon was brought before the Court of Burgomaster and Schepens, upon the complaint of the Schout or Sheriff, for keeping open his store on Sunday, during the sermon, and selling at retail; the complainant demanding that he should be deprived of his trade, and condemned to pay a fine of six hundred guilders, at that time a very heavy sum to impose upon any one in the little colony. The accused, not understanding the nature of the charge brought against him, a copy of it in writing was delivered to him with instruction to appear upon the next court day. The Sheriff then informed the court that the Governor and Council had resolved that the Jews who had come in the preceding autumn as well as those that had recently arrived from Holland, must prepare to depart forthwith; that they would receive notice thereof, and the Sheriff asked if the court, which was also a council for the municipal government of the city, had any objection to make; whereupon, says the record, it was decided that the Governor's resolution should take its course. (10)

---

10. The following is the record of the hearing:
"Monday, 1st March, 1655.
In the City Hall
Present,
    The Heeren
        Allart. Anthony,
        Oloff Stevenson,
        Cornelis Van Tienhoven,
        Johannes Verbrugge,
        Johannes Nevius,
        Johannes de Peyster,
        Jacob Striker and
        Van Vinge.
Cornelis Van Tienhoven, in quality of Sheriff of this City, Plaintiff,
vs.
Abram De La Simon, a Jew, Defendant.
Plaintiff rendering his demand in writing, saying that he, De La Simon, hath kept his store open during the sermon, and sold by

This notice, I presume, was given, as some left, for their number appears to have diminished. Others, however, remained, the Governor's course being arrested by the order received from Holland. (11) Fortunately for those who departed, there was one

---

retail, as proved by affidavit, concluding therefore, that Defendant shall be deprived of 'his trade and condemned in a fine of 600 guilders. The charge having been read before Defendant, who not understanding the same, it was ordered that a copy be given Defendant to answer the same before next Court Day. The Heer Cornelis Van Tienhoven informed the Burgomaster and Schepens that the Director General and Supreme Council have resolved that the Jews who came here last year from the West Indies and now from Fatherland, must prepare to depart forthwith, and that they shall receive notice thereof, and asked if the Burgomaster and Schepens had anything to object thereto. It was decided, not; but that the resolution relating thereto should take its course."—Valentine's Manual for 1849, p. 387.

Before this order could be carried out, the orders from Holland to the contrary probably arrived, as will presently appear. The best proof of this is that the names of all of these early Jewish immigrants appear in the official records frequently and continuously subsequent to the date of this order.

I have ventured to add the following amusing incident, also bearing on the observance of the Sunday in early New York, which gives evidence of the changed condition of affairs a century and a half later: "A story is related of a respectable Jew at New York, who, through the malice of a powerful neighbor, was chosen constable, an office which the former endeavored to be excused from serving. The first Sunday of his entering upon his office, he seated himself on a stool before his door, and every servant that went by to fetch water, he took the pails from. He also interrupted, as far as in his power, every kind of work on the *Sabbath day*, and so annoyed his enemy and the rest of the neighborhood with the severity of his regulations, that they were glad to substitute another in his place."—A Description of the City of New York, 1807-8, by John Lambert. Valentine's Manual for 1870, p. 864.—EDITOR.

11. On the 13th of March, 1656, the Directors wrote a letter to Stuyvesant, containing the following: "The permission given to the Jews to go to New Netherland and enjoy the same privileges, as

spot in America where universal toleration was recognized: the little colony founded by Roger Williams in Rhode Island. A fugitive himself from persecution, Roger Williams had laid down as a fundamental principle of his commonwealth the sanctity of conscience; that the civil magistrate should restrain crime but not control opinions; that he should punish guilt but never violate the freedom of the soul—a doctrine, says Bancroft, which was an entire reformation of theological jurisprudence, and gave equal protection to every form of religious faith. In 1652, two years before the arrival of these Jewish emigrants, the colony of Rhode Island enacted that

---

they have here (in Amsterdam), has been granted only as far as civil and political rights are concerned, without giving the said Jews a claim to the privilege of exercising their religion in a synagogue or a gathering; so long, therefore, as you receive no request for granting them this liberty of religious exercise, your considerations and anxiety about this matter are premature, and when later something shall be said about it, you can do no better than to refer them to us, and await the necessary order. Your next remark concerning trade does not as yet divert us from our resolution."

Again, on the 14th of June, 1656, they wrote: "We have seen and heard with displeasure, that against our orders of the 15th day of February, 1655, issued at the request of the Jewish or Portuguese nation, you have forbidden them to trade to Fort Orange and the South River, also the purchase of real estate, which is granted to them without difficulty here in this country, and we wish it had not been done, and that you had obeyed our orders, which you must always execute punctually and with more respect. Jews or Portuguese people, however, shall not be employed in any public service (to which they are neither admitted in this city), nor allowed to have open retail shops, but they may quietly and peacefully carry on their business as beforesaid and exercise in all quietness their religion within their houses, for which end they must without doubt endeavor to build their houses close together in a convenient place on one or the other side of New Amsterdam—at their choice—as they have done here."—Documents Relating to the Colonial History of the State of New York. Vol. XIV, pp. 341, 351 respectively.—EDITOR "all men of whatever nation soever they may be, that shall be received inhabitants of any of the towns, shall have the same privileges as Englishmen, any law to the contrary notwithstanding," which was both a general act of naturalization to all who came within that colony, as well as a recognition of the privilege of all to the equal enjoyment of civil rights.

It is my impression that those who departed went to Rhode Island. The Rhode Island historians say (11a) that the Jews came to Newport, R. I., as early as 1657; that they were of Dutch extraction; that they came from the island of Curacoa; that they were not possessed of the wealth, intelligence or enterprise which so eminently distinguished those who settled in Newport afterwards, and in the very year mentioned by these historians, 1657, an event occurred in Rhode Island, which pointed it out as the place for all who sought the sacred enjoyment of civil and religious liberty.

The persecuted Quakers had full refuge there, and the commissioners of the United Colonies remonstrated with the President of that colony for protecting this troublesome sect. The answer given to this remonstrance was, that "persecution only tended to increase sects," and that they had no law in Rhode Island "for preventing any one from declaring by words their mind or understanding concerning the ways or the things of God," one of the noblest expositions ever given of religious freedom. From these circumstances and the proximity of Rhode Island, I infer that some of the Jewish emigrants left New Amsterdam and settled in Newport, between the years 1655 and 1657, and that they were afterwards joined by others who came directly from Cura-

---

11 a. Peterson's History, of R. I., p. 181.

coa. There were at that time vessels trading between Curacoa and New Amsterdam, and as the scheme for a Jewish colony at the former place had, after two years of time, proved abortive, and the affairs of the island were otherwise not prosperous, the probability is that some of the Jews, who had gone out there, left, and coming as they naturally would on the return passage to New Amsterdam, and being there informed of the advantages presented by Rhode Island, that they joined their coreligionists in that colony, and with those previously there, became the nucleus of the wealthy and influential Jewish community, which continued to expand and flourish in Newport until some time after the American revolution.

Of the Jews who remained in New York, then called New Amsterdam, the most prominent or leading man appears to have been Abraham D'Lucena, as his name generally appears first in the several applications made in behalf of himself and his brethren to Stuyvesant's government. In July, 1655, he applied, with several others, for a burying ground, but the request was rudely refused, the reply being, "that there was no need for it yet." (12) Death, however, says O'Callaghan, soon removed this excuse, and on the 14th of July, 1656, a lot was granted to them on the outside of the city "for a place of interment." The exact place outside the city, where the first burial place of the Jewish race in North America was, has not been positively ascertained. It is my impression, for reasons that will be

---

12. Calendar of Historical Manuscripts. Edited by E. B. O'Callaghan. Dutch Manuscripts. Council Minutes, p. 150.
Burial ground granted, Feb. 22d, 1656. Do. p. 160, O'Callaghan's date seems erroneous.—EDITOR.

stated hereafter, that it was on the side of a ridge of elevated ground near the southerly side of the present site of Oliver Street, west of Madison and near Henry Street.

At the period 1655, the position of the city was perilous. It was exposed to attacks from Spanish cruisers and pirates, and to assaults from the Indians, who had been badly treated by the Dutch governors, and were enemies. The encroachments of the English, moreover, in Long Island and Westchester, was the subject of constant anxiety, England never having conceded the right of the Dutch to settle New Netherland, and there was an apprehension of what afterwards occurred, the capture of the place by the English. This being the state of things, all the male inhabitants, capable of bearing arms, were enrolled in what was called the Burgher Guard, for the protection and defence of the city, and a watch was kept up night and day with the steadiness and vigilance of a beleaguered town. A few months after the arrival of these Jewish emigrants, the question arose whether the adult males among them should be incorporated in the Burgher Guard; the officer of the guard submitting the question to the Governor and Council. It was duly deliberated upon and an ordinance was passed which, after reciting the unwillingness "of the mass of the citizens" to be fellow-soldiers "of the aforesaid nation," or watch in the same guardhouse, and the fact that the Jews in Holland did not serve in the trainbands of the cities, but paid a compensation for their exemption therefrom, declared that they should be exempt from this military service, and that for such exemption each male person between the ages of 16 and 60 should pay a monthly contribution of sixty-five stivers. (13)

---

13. Resolution to exempt the Jews from military service, 28th of August, (1655):

This was not absolute, and, accordingly, two of them, Jacob Barsimson and Asser Levy, petitioned to be allowed to stand guard like the other burghers, or to be relieved from the tax imposed upon their nation, which was refused by the Governor and Council with the curt addition, that "they might go elsewhere if they liked." (14) Neither of them, how-

---

The Captains and officers of the trainbands of this city having asked the Director General and Council, whether the Jewish people, who reside in this city, should also train and mount guard with the citizens' bands, this was taken in consideration and deliberated upon: first the disgust and unwillingness of these trainbands to be fellow-soldiers with the aforesaid nation and to be on guard with them in the same guard house, and on the other side, that the said nation was not admitted or counted among the citizens, as regards trainbands or common citizens' guards, neither in the illustrious City of Amsterdam nor (to our knowledge) in any city in Netherland; but in order that the said nation may honestly be taxed for their freedom in that respect, it is directed by the Director General and Council to prevent further discontent, that the aforesaid nation shall, according to the usages of the renowned City of Amsterdam, remain exempt from the general training and guard duty, on condition that each male person over 16 and under 60 years contribute for the aforesaid freedom towards the relief of the general municipal taxes 65 stivers [$1.30] every month, and the military council of the citizens is hereby authorized and charged to carry this into effect until our further orders, and to collect pursuant to the above, the aforesaid contribution once in every month, and in case of refusal, to collect it by legal process. Thus done in Council at Fort Amsterdam, on the day as above.

(It was signed):

P. Stuyvesant,
Nicasius De Sille,
Cornelis Van Tienhoven.

(Vol. XII, p. 96, Documents Relating to Colonial History, etc.)—EDITOR

14. Calendar of Historical Manuscripts. Do. Council Minutes, p. 151. November 5, 1655.

Asser Levy's name appears more frequently, probably, than that of any other Jewish settler of this time, in the official records. He

ever, had any such disposition, for Barsimson's name appears subsequently as a litigant in the courts, and Asser Levy, who was a butcher, became afterwards a prominent man in the colony, and was distinguished from the beginning for the pertinacity with which he insisted upon the rights of himself and his brethren.

In December of the same year, 1655, one of their number, Salvator D'Andrada, who was also a merchant, purchased at auction a house and lot in the city, but when he came to pay the purchase money, an objection was raised as to his right to acquire and hold real estate. He accordingly petitioned the Governor and council, praying that he might be allowed to take a deed, being ready to pay the purchase money. His application was refused for, says the record, "pregnant reasons." The owner then petitioned that he might be allowed to convey his house and lot to D'Andrada, or, if not that the Governor and council would take it in virtue of their right of pre-emption, and pay the price. But this was also refused, the sale was declared void and the property was afterwards sold to another person. (15)

Abraham D'Lucena, then, together with four of his brethren, presented March 14th, 1656, a formal petition, setting forth that they and their coreligionists were assessed the same as other citizens, and

---

seems to have been extremely active and to have held even certain public offices. A long article of interest can be written about him alone.—EDITOR.

15. Calendar of Historical Manuscripts do. pp. 156, 157.

By the order of the 14th of June, 1656, from the Directors to Stuyvesant (see Note 11), the Jews were expressly given permission to own real estate, and Stuyvesant was censured for having prevented them from so doing. Subsequently to this, they seem to have had no difficulties about this matter.—EDITOR.

asking that they should have in common with others the same right to trade and to hold real estate, according to the act of the Amsterdam directors of February 15th, 1655. (16) They were not only assessed with the other tax-paying inhabitants, but, as appears from the records, very heavily, at least those mentioned in the petition. In the preceding year, 1655, a tax was imposed to defray the cost of erecting the outer fence, or city wall, from which the present Wall Street takes it name. For this these five petitioners were assessed each 1,000 florins, being the same amount imposed upon the wealthiest of the citizens, and two-thirds of the amount assessed upon the Governor, as the representative of the company, showing that they were either among the wealthiest of the inhabitants, or were very unequally taxed.

Abm. D'Lucena, then and for many years afterwards a merchant in the city, together with several of his brethren, put goods on board a ship bound for the Delaware river, claiming that under the Act of the Amsterdam Chamber of Feb. 15th, 1655, they had a general right to trade, and on the 29th of November, 1655, they petitioned the Governor that they might have the right to trade to the Delaware,

---

16. Calendar of Historical Manuscripts do. p. 162. The names of the petitioners were: Abraham de Lucena, Jacob Cohen Henricque, Salvator Dandrada, Joseph D'Coster and David Frera, The Directors and Council answered that they awaited further instructions from Holland, which were received soon after in the letter of 14th June, 1656, mentioned in the last note and found in Note 11.

The assessment list may be found in Valentine's History of the City of New York, pp. 315-8. It includes the following names and amounts in currency of the present day: Abraham La Cuya, (Lucena?), $40; Joseph d'Costar, $40; David Frera, $40; Fusilador Dandrade, $40; Jacob Cowyn, $40; Jacob Barsimson, $3.—
EDITOR.

(the Southriver) and to Albany, (Fort Orange). The privilege to trade as requested was refused, but they were allowed to forward the goods they had shipped, with the understanding, however, that it was not to be taken as a precedent and their general application was referred "to Fatherland," that is, to the Directors of the West India Company, or the portion of them known as the Amsterdam Chamber (17).

---

17. This petition is found below, as well as an account of the deliberations upon it:

"To the Honorable Worshipful Director General and Council of New Netherlands show with due reverence, (name) for themselves and in the name of others of the Jewish nation, residing in that city, that under date of the 15th of February, 1655, they, the petitioners, have from the Honorable Lords Directors of the Incorporated West India Company, Masters and Patrons of the Province, received permission and consent to travel, reside and trade here like the other inhabitants and enjoy the same liberties, which is proved by the document here annexed. They request therefore respectfully, that your Noble Worships will not prevent or hinder them herein but will allow and consent that, pursuant to their permit, they may, with other inhabitants of this Province, travel to and trade on the South River of New Netherland, at Fort Orange and other places, situate within the jurisdiction of this Government of New Netherland. So doing etc., they shall remain your Noble Worships'
       humble servants,
Signed,   Abraham de Lucena,
       Salvator Dandrada,
       Jacob Coen."

After the foregoing petition had been read, at the meeting of the Director General and Council, it was resolved, that each of the members of the Council should give his opinion as to what answer is to be made:

Opinion of the Honorable Director General, Petrus Stuyvesant: "To answer, that the petition is to be denied for weighty reasons."

Opinion of the Honorable Nicasius de Sille:

He says, that "he does not like to act herein contrary to the orders of the Lords Directors, but that at present, as they have put on board ship goods for the Southriver, permission might be given to them, and further orders in answer to the last letter sent to the Lords Directors, should be awaited."

The constant hostility of Stuyvesant, and his persistent efforts to deprive them of what they would have enjoyed in Holland, was in itself a cause for inducing others to remove to Rhode Island, and no doubt did contribute to increase the numbers of those who settled in Newport. Those who remained undoubtedly communicated to their influential brethren in Holland, the treatment they continued to receive at the hands of Stuyvesant. For on the 13th of March, 1656, the Directors wrote to Stuyvesant, that the consent given that they might go to New Netherland and enjoy there "the same liberty their nation enjoyed in Holland included all the civil

---

Opinion of the Honorable Lamontagne.
"To answer, that for weighty reasons, the petition is denied."

Opinion of the Honorable Cornelis van Tienhoven, written by himself:

"Cornelis van Tienhoven is of opinion under correction, that to grant the petition of the Jews for permission to go to the Southriver and Fort Orange, although the noble Lords Directors had allowed this nation to live and trade in New Netherland, would nevertheless be very injurious to the community and population of the said places, and therefore the petition must be denied for the coming winter, and ample report be made thereon to the Lords Directors, also that for this time a young man of that nation may be allowed to go to the Southriver with some goods, without thereby establishing a precedent."

" Petition of Abraham de Lucena and other Jews for permission to trade on the South River, etc.," Documents relating to Colonial History, XII. pp. 117, 118, 29th November, 1655.

This last opinion appears to have been adopted, for an order was issued that "for weighty reasons is the request expressed in general terms declined, but as we are informed the suppliants have embarked already some goods thither, so are they now permitted to send two persons towards Southriver to trade with them, and when they shall have disposed of their goods, then to return hither."—Albany Records, Vol. X., p. 178, quoted in Hazard's Annals of Pa p. 205. Calendar of Historical Manuscripts, etc., p. 156.—EDITOR.

and religious privileges," and when the Amsterdam Chamber were advised of the Governor's refusal to allow them to trade, the Chamber, June 14th, 1656, expressed its dissatisfaction by letter in very strong terms, in these words: "We have observed with displeasure that, contrary to our concessions, granted on the 15th of February, 1655, to the *Jews* or *Portuguese* nation, you have forbidden them to trade to Fort Orange (18), and to the South-river (19), or to purchase real estate which is here allowed without any difficulty," and then, after declaring their wish, that the Governor ought more respectfully to follow their orders and obey them according to their tenor, the letter added: "The Jews

---

18. Shortly after this, on December 28th. 1655, we find Isaac Israel and Benjamin Cardoso among the traders on the Delaware with Vice-Director Jean Paul Jacquet. In spite of the terms of the order in the note above, or more properly in consequence of the letter from the Directors, no difficulties seem to have been placed in the way of Jews settling permanently here. In 1663, we find that Israel was a member of the High Council of the Director of the D. W. I. Co's. colony on the South River (Delaware River). In 1680, we find a Mr. Isaack and Richard Levey among the responsible house-keepers near the Delaware River. These facts are of unusual interest, because they indicate that Jews settled in the present State of Delaware at New Castle and elsewhere at such an early date. My authorities are given at some length in Appendix I.—EDITOR.

19. Jews seemed to have availed themselves of permission to trade at Fort Orange, (Albany) at a very early date. This is evidenced by references to Asser Levy engaging in purchases of merchandise and real estate in Albany in 1661. See "Early Records of the City and County of Albany", by J. Pearson, pp. 297, 308 309, 362. 371, 372, 376, 381; as appears from the text, the family of Asser Levy, after his death, settled on Long Island, making another early Jewish settlement.

In August, 1678, we also find Jacob Lucena petitioning for a pass to go to Albany and Esopus to trade.—Calendar of Historical manuscripts.—EDITOR.

or Portuguese nation are not, however, to be at liberty to exercise any handicraft or to keep any open retail store, which they cannot do in this city. But they shall pursue peaceably and quietly their commerce as aforesaid, and be at liberty to exercise their religious worship in all quietness within their houses."

After the letter was received, Asser Levy applied to the Court of Burgomaster and Schepens to admit him to the right of citizenship, and exhibited his certificate to the Court to show that he had been a burgher in Amsterdam; but his request was not complied with. Salvator D'Andrada, and others also made a similar application (20) and were refused, whereupon they brought the matter before the Governor and Council, and as the directions from Holland were controlling, an order was made April 21st, 1657, that the Burgomaster should admit them to that privilege. Here the struggle virtually ended, and they were no longer troubled during the Dutch rule. The names of these early emigrants, so far as they can now be gathered from the records, are as follows: Abraham D'Lucena, David Israel, Moses Ambrosius, Abraham De La Simon, Salvator D'Andrada, Joseph Da Costa, David Frera, Jacob Barsimson, Jacob C. Henricque, or as it was sometimes written, Jacob Cohen, Isaac Mesa, and Asser Levy, nearly all of whom would seem from the names to have been of Portuguese or Spanish origin.

Abraham D'Lucena is the person to whom I referred in the beginning in connection with an act of charity. A vessel, purporting to be a Spanish privateer, but commanded by a Dutchman, captured a Spanish vessel upon the ocean, and brought the

---

20. The Market Book, p. 50. Calendar of Historical Manuscripts, etc., p. 184.

cargo, consisting of twenty-seven negroes and merchandise, to New Amsterdam, where he disposed of the negroes among the inhabitants in exchange for other commodities. The owner of the negroes applied to Holland for restitution, and the Dutch government directed the authorities in New Amsterdam, to see that justice was done to him. He accordingly came out to the colony but could get no satisfaction, and through his long waiting having exhausted his means, and been reduced to a state of great destitution, he was supported for some time by the authorities, as he complained, in a very insufficient manner, and Lucena paid his passage to enable him to return to Europe. (21) A descendant of Lucena, was living in 1759, and his son, as I presume from the name, Abraham D'Lucena, was the second Jewish minister or preacher in the first synagogue erected in this city.

The city was captured by the English in 1664, and its name changed to New York. For half a century afterwards, very little is to be found respecting the Jewish residents. Their increase in numbers was very moderate, for the reason probably that few of their persuasion emigrated to the colony, after the government passed into the hands of the English. In 1683, an act was passed by the Colonial Assembly for the naturalization of foreigners; but it offered no advantage to them as it was limited to those professing Christianity. (22).

In 1685, Saul Brown, a merchant who had come from Newport and settled in New York, complained to Governor Dongan, by petition, that he had been

---

21. The date of this incident is 1657. See Documents relating to Colonial History of the State of New York, Vol. II., p. 39.—EDITOR.

22. Parker's Laws of New York, 112.

interfered with in his trade under an existing municipal regulation. The Governor referred Brown's petition to the Mayor and Common Council, who declared that no Jew could sell by retail in the city, but might by wholesale, if the Governor thought fit to permit it. (23). There was a previous regulation that none but burghers or freemen could sell by retail, and this was equivalent to holding that no Jew could become a burgher or freeman of the city. The privilege to sell by wholesale, however, must have been conceded to Brown, for he was for many years afterwards a prominent merchant.

In 1683, a Charter of Liberties and Privileges was adopted by the colonial legislature, which among other provisions, declared that "no one should be molested, punished, disquieted, or called in question for his religious opinions, who *professed faith in God, by Jesus Christ*," but that all such persons should "at all times freely have and enjoy their judgments and consciences in matters of religion throughout the province," which was extending religious freedom to all but Jews. This Charter was regarded as a great public triumph, and the inhabitants of the city were summoned by sound of trumpet to assemble and hear it publicly read in front of the City Hall, in presence of all the city and colonial authorities.

Two years afterwards, 1685, the Jewish residents, who must have heard a great deal about the religious freedom secured by this charter, petitioned Governor Dongan "for liberty to exercise their religion," probably unaware that the provision in the charter did not apply to them, or, perhaps, supposing that the Governor had power independent of this pro-

---

23. 2 Dunlop, Appendix cxxxiv, Booth's History of New York, p. 198, 2 Brod., p, 426.

vincial statute. In the formal written instructions of James, Duke of York, afterwards James II., to Governor Andros, who had succeeded Dongan, the Governor was required "to permit all persons of what religion soever, quietly to inhabit within the government, and to give no disturbance or disquiet whatsoever for or by reason of their differing in matters of religion." But this important provision was left out in the written instructions to Governor Dongan, which may have been the reason for his adopting the course which he did, which was to refer the petition to the Mayor and Common Council of New York, by whom it was considered, and their decision is recorded in these words: "that no public worship is tolerated by act of assembly, but to those that profess faith in Christ, and therefore the Jew's worship not to be allowed."

When James, however, became king, a new copy of instructions was, in 1686, sent out to Dongan, in which this important promise was re-inserted, and they may have led to what afterwards took place, for it is certain that the Jews had a synagogue as early as 1695 and may have it in 1691, for La Motthe Cadillac, in his account of New York in 1691, enumerates the Jews as one of the sects and then says that each sect had its church and freedom of religion. (24). Dongan, who was one of the best Governors the colony ever had, was a very liberal-minded man, and it is very probable that he may, when his new instructions came out with this clause restored, have granted to the Jewish residents this privilege they asked, or it may, in consequence of the restoration of the particular clause, have been conceded during the temporary rule of Leisler, or by

---

24 Colonial Documents, ix., 549.

the succeeding Governors, Sloughter or Fletcher. (25).

The synagogue referred to, which I suppose to have been the first upon the Continent of North America, was on the south side of the present Beaver Street, in the middle of the block, between Broadway and Broad Street. Its existence in 1695 and its location are established by a description of New York, written by the Rev. John Miller, Chaplain to the English garrison, to which description he affixed a plan or map of the city, in which the position of the public buildings and especially all the religious edifices, is carefully indicated as they existed in 1695.

In the text of the work, Miller gave a tabular statement of the different religious denominations, the number of each, and the name of the minister; from which it appears that the Jewish congregation consisted of twenty families and the name of the minister was Saul Brown. This was the merchant already referred to, who in 1685 was allowed the burgher privileges and, as he was carrying on business in 1685 as a merchant, and for several years afterwards, it is presumed that he was not a regular minister, but what is known in Jewish congregations as a reader. The building used as a synagogue must, from the indications upon the map, have been a small one.

---

25. In the volume for 1885 of the New York Historical Society Collections, the names of two Jews, Isaac Henriquez and Simon Bonan, appear on the rolls of Freemen, in 1687-8 and others subsequently, so that Dongan, or one of his immediate successors, appears to have swept away this discrimination against the Jews, of which Samuel Brown complained. Besides in 1683, permission had been granted to Joseph Bueno and others, whom we know to have been Jewish, "to trade and traffic within the city of New York."—Calendar of Historical Manuscripts—Eng. Man. p. 154.— EDITOR.

It was possibly nothing more than an ordinary house, converted into a place for public worship, as was the case at the time in respect to the religious edifices of the several other of the smaller denominations. It is represented on the map as corresponding with the building in the next street to it, used by the French Protestants, which was a very humble edifice. Saul Brown was succeeded by Abraham D'Lucena. Lucena was also a merchant. It appears, however, that in 1710, he petitioned Governor Hunter, to be exempted, as minister for the Jews, from all offices and duties, civil and military (26). I cannot say whether this application was granted or not, but he carried on business afterwards as a merchant, having been concerned with others in furnishing provisions for the expedition against Canada in 1711. (27).

When Lord Bellamont was Governor in 1698, he had arrayed against him the leading merchants in consequence of his efforts to put down the piracy connived at by his predecessors, and was also opposed by the aristocratic party, because he had disapproved of their course in the trial and execution of Leisler. The aristocratic and mercantile class combined together, so as to deprive him of the pecuniary means necessary to carry on his government, and so extensive and powerful was this combination, that he writes in 1700 to the Lords of Trade: "Were it not for one Dutch merchant and two or three Jews that have let me have money, I should have been undone." (28).

In the beginning of this century, 1700, a very profitable commerce was carried on between New

---

26. Calendar of Historical Manuscripts. English Manuscripts, p. 373. This petition is reprinted in Documentary History of the State of New York. Vol. III., p. 434.
27. Calendar of Historical Manuscripts. Eng. MSS., p. 391.
28. Colonial Documents, iv., p. 720.

York and the West Indies, in which several of the Jewish merchants were engaged, and there being great scarcity in Europe about the close of the French war, wheat was exported from New York to Lisbon. Though this trade was of short duration it proved exceedingly profitable to those engaged in it, so that several of them were enabled to purchase estates. (29). Two of the merchants engaged in this traffic to Lisbon were Abraham D'Lucena and Louis Gomez, and as they were afterward two of the most affluent of the Jewish residents, it may be supposed that they were among the fortunate in this Lisbon trade, which could not be maintained when the price of wheat fell in Europe, as the vessels obtained no cargos upon their return voyage to New York.

Though this direct trade between New York and Portugal was, as I have said, of short duration, it was attended by an increase in the Jewish population both in New York and Newport, and I infer, that the vessels engaged in it brought Jewish passengers upon the return voyage, some of whom remained in New York whilst others settled in Newport. I infer this, as new names undoubtedly of Spanish or Portuguese origin appear about this period for the first time among the Jewish residents. (30).

---

29. Valentine's Manual, 1852.

30. In this connection, it is interesting to notice that even at this early period the various nationalities of Europe seem to have been pretty well represented among the Jewish inhabitants of New York City. Some evidence of this fact is found in the following passage from a letter which appears in the New York Historical Society Collections for 1880, p. 342. It appears that one of the clergy of the city, the Rev. John Sharpe, proposed that a School Library and Chapel be erected in New York City, in 1712-3. Some of the advantages which the city offered for that purpose are pointed by him as follows: "It is possible also to learn Hebrew here as well as in Europe, there being a synagogue of Jews, and

One of the principal personages in the Jewish community at this period was Louis Gomez, who emigrated from England to New York about the commencement of this century and died in 1730. He had five sons: Mordecai, Daniel, David, Isaac and Benjamin. Mordecai was associated with his father in mercantile business and became the head of the house upon his father's death. He was, until his death in 1750, one of the principal merchants of New York, and the accession of this Gomez family, who were men of intelligence and of high character, proved a very material addition to the little Jewish community, of which they were for many years the recognized head. (31).

The Synagogue in Beaver Street was now found to be too small or of too humble a character for a denomination, who, though limited in numbers, were as a body both wealthy and influential. (32). It was

---

many ingenious men of that nation from Poland, Hungary, Germany, etc."—EDITOR.

31. The above remarks are based on numerous references to the family in the colonial annals. These and many other similar statements show how large and varied the commercial relations of the Jews of New York were at this early period. There were vessels owned wholly or in part by Jews plying between New York and various points in South America and the West Indies, Europe, Asia and even Africa. When these papers and other data, including commissions of vessels, clearance papers, bills of lading, etc, have been collected (many of them are in the Brodhead collection in Albany and need merely be copied and translated), we will have ample material for an elaborate article on the commerce of the Jews of New York from 1655 to the Revolution, and I believe such an article will not only awaken interest but also great surprise, because of the magnitude of the commerce in question. My own investigations, chiefly in connection with the Documents Relating to the Colonial History of New York, amply warrant these assertions. —EDITOR.

32. The text has contained several references to this congre-

accordingly given up in about 1728, and a new synagogue was erected in a different part of the city. This was what was afterwards known as the Mill Street Synagogue, and as the street where it stood has now disappeared in consequence of the changes made in that part of the city after the fire of 1855, it may be of interest to give some account of the locality of this synagogue, which for more than a century was the only one in New York.

Mill Street was a small narrow street, running out of Broad Street in a north-easterly direction for a short distance, and then suddenly terminating in a narrow lane which ran south into 'Stone Street. The part extending from Broad Street was about or

---

gation in the preceding pages. There seems to be but scanty data about its history prior to the beginning of the Eighteenth century. The following will somewhat supplement Judge Daly's remarks. It is based on a communication to the Historical Magazine, Vol. I., p. 366, of Series III., from Rev. Dr. A. Fischell, then a colleague of Rabbi Raphall, of this city: The first minutes of this congregation are in Spanish, beginning in 1729, and have references to certain wholesome rules and regulations made about the year 1706, by the Elders of the Congregation "to preserve peace, tranquility and good government among them and those after them." The following names are affixed;

Moses Gomez, Daniel Gomez, Benjamin Mendes Pacheco, Abraham Riviero, Mordecai Gomez, Nathan Levy, Isaac d'Medena, Joseph Nunez, Doctor Nunez, D. Costa, Abraham Franks, Baruch Juda, Jacob Franks, and Moses Gomez, Jr. Ten years later the following names were added: J. Myers Cohen, David Gomez, J. R. Rodriguez, Judah Hays, Judah Mears and Solomon Hays.

The list of names of early Jewish residents given thus far is not by any means to be considered complete. A number of families which arrived here in the seventeenth century seem to have either migrated or become extinct by this time. (1729). There are references to a number of others not yet mentioned, in my possession, but as a couple of them are doubtful and the list cannot be deemed complete, I shall dismiss the subject with this explanation.—EDITOR.

very near the line of the present South William Street, and the little lane or alley where it ended, still remains, running from South William to Stone Street. It was one of the most secluded and quiet streets in the city, and so narrow at either entrance that it might have been passed without recognizing it as a thoroughfare. During the Dutch occupation it was known as the Sluyk Steegie, or miry lane, from the fact that the drainage of the hilly or elevated land which then extended from Hanover Square to near the corner of Exchange Place and Broad Street, ran into this little valley or open way, which was difficult of passage and had but a few straggling houses of a very humble character.

At the upper end of it from Broad Street, there was a copious spring of fresh water which at an early period of the settlement supplied a tannery, and near this tannery was a horse-mill for grinding the bark, from which the locality took its name. At a later period this spring turned a water-mill, from which there was a cartway from Broad Street, long known as Mill Lane, whilst from the rear of the mill the short narrow lane, which is still existing, ran into Stone Street, then one of the principal streets of the city. In 1663, Asser Levy, previously mentioned as one of the first emigrants, purchased two lots in the part known as Mill Lane, alongside of a house and lot belonging to another Jewish resident, Daniel Joghimsen (probably Joachimsen), the lots bought by Levy being located, as I infer, from the deed, in about the place where the second or Mill Street Synagogue was built, and very near the spring which supplied the water-mill referred to. Grant Thorburn, when he came to New York in 1794, conversed with a very old man who remembered the mill, the wheel of which was turned by the water from the spring, and he,

Thorburn, adds, that the reason assigned for the Jews erecting their synagogue in this place, was "because of its vicinity to the waters of the spring-water being much used upon their day of purification," (33) and Watson records that he heard from the Phillips family that, when the Jews first held their worship in Mill Street, "they had a living spring in which they were accustomed to perform their ablutions and cleansings according to the rites of their religion (34).

Asser Levy, who purchased this property in Mill Street, was one of the sworn butchers of this city, who some years afterwards became the proprietor of a celebrated tavern just within the water gate at the bottom of Wall Street, on the outside of which gate he had a slaughter-house, which he had been permitted to erect by the authorities, as a place for slaughtering cattle for the general use of all persons in the city. He died in 1682, when his family removed to Long Island. (35). He was an active, energetic man, who had acquired considerable property, and the land, upon which the Mill Street Synagogue was built about 1728, was probably obtained from his heirs, either by gift or purchase.

The new synagogue received the name of Shearith Israel, *Remnant of Israel*. It was a small stone structure, very plain without, but very neat within. (36). It was separated from the street by a wooden paling, having a gate at the eastern end, and the entrance to the synagogue was in the rear. (37).

Nearly three quarters of an century had now elapsed

---

33. Reminiscences of Grant Thorburn. p. 212, N. J. 1845.
34. Dunlap's history of New York. p. 484.
35. De Voe's Market Book, pp. 45, 46, 54, 55.
36. Smith's History of New York.
37. There is a drawing of the building upon the map made by David Grim of the city, as it existed in 1746.

since the arrival of the first and the emigrants burial ground being full, measures were taken contemporaneous with the erection of this synagogue, for procuring a new burial place. It appears by the records that on the 26th of July, 1727, a conveyance was made to Louis Gomez, trustee, by Isaac Levy, Asher Nathan Levy, Isaac Levy, Judah Mears and Jacob Franks, executors of Moses Levy, of two lots of ground in "the street commonly known as the Gold Street", marked No. 84 and 85 in the map of the division of the lands of William Beekman, for the consideration of £46, 13s. money, "raised" in the language of the deed, "by voluntary subscriptions of the inhabitants of New York of the Jewish religion;" which two lots by the terms of the conveyance were "to be and remain forever thereafter, a burial place for the habitants of the city of New York, being of the Jewish religion, and to and for no other use, intent, or purpose whatsoever." These two lots, which had together a front of 50 feet by 112 deep, were on the easterly side of the present Gold Street, between Ferry and Beekman Streets, and I have been thus particular in describing the conveyance of them, as it is necessary in connection with what will be hereafter stated to show where the old burial ground was.

This property having been obtained, a petition signed by Louis Gomez and eleven others was, on the 23d of August, 1728, presented to the Common Council, setting forth that the "inhabitants of the City of New York of the Jewish religion" had "some years since purchased a small piece of land beyond the Fresh Water for a burying place," that the "said burying place was then full," and that "they would have purchased some more land adjourning thereto, but it being in dispute, they could not obtain any title to it;" that they "were consequently obliged to purchase lots of land lying near the Cripple Bush or swamp, but would not presume to make a burying place thereof without the leave of the Common Council;" which petition closed with the request that permission would be given, and the application was granted.

From circumstances which afterwards occurred, these two lots were never used for the purpose for which they had been bought, and as an explanation of what subsequently transpired will show very clearly where the first burial ground was, I will give the facts with more minuteness of detail than would otherwise have been called for, as a portion of this old burial ground still remains, and it may be interesting to know that the small piece of land in the New Bowery, below Oliver Street, now enclosed from the street by an iron railing and kept as an old Jewish grave-yard, is a part of what was the first burial place of the Jewish race in North America.

It will be remembered that I stated that the order made in 1656, granting the Jews a burial-ground, refers to the place as "outside the City." There was at that time but one road leading outside the City. There was an open or clear space beyond the City Wall, but this, as a locality, was generally referred to in deeds and other documents, as "outside the City gate." It did not reach very far, and beyond it a dense forest extended for nearly two miles in the direction of Chatham Square; whilst the land to the West, between this wood and the Hudson River, was broken up by low irregular hills, swamps, marshes, and large deposits of water. The road referred to as leading "outside the City," began at the water gate, about the corner of the present Wall and Pearl Streets for at that time the water of the East River reached up as far as Pearl Street, and the road ran along the edge of the water to what is now Fulton street. At this point it turned, running along in about the direction of the present Pearl Street, to its junction with Chatham Street, when it extended up Chatham street and up the Bowery to Harlem. What is now Chatham Square, was then the southern limit of a range of high hills, or perhaps more properly, an elevated plateau, extending on the one side as far as the point where Mulberry Street intersects Canal Street, whilst on the easterly side of Chatham Square, this line of hills curved across the present Oliver and Catherine Streets, towards Monroe Street and then ran along what is now very nearly the line of Monroe Street to Rutgers Street. This elevated land, which extended northerly in the direction of Harlem, being in the early settlement well adapted for cultivation whilst the meadows below it and east of it, that is, between it and the East River, being highly prized by the Dutch for the pasturing of cattle, the whole was parcelled among the early settlers into farms, or as the Dutch called them, Bouweries, a word that has survived in the name of the present street, the Bowery, which was originally the road leading through these Bouweries in the direction of Harlem. These farms, or Bouweries, were at first leased out by the Dutch Governor, to the original settlers, but being exposed to attacks from the Indians, and having been twice devastated by the savages, they were almost deserted about the time of the arrival of the first Jewish emigrants in 1654. It was to this locality, afterwards known as Batavia, that the descriptive words "outside the City," in the order allowing the Jews a place of burial appropriately applied in 1656, and that this was the place where the first burial ground stood, I will now proceed to show.

Within the space now bounded by Broadway, Canal, Mulberry, Chatham and Reade Streets, there was a lake of considerable extent called by the Dutch "The Kollock," and by the English, "The Fresh Water," which had an outlet into the East River, by a small stream called the "Oulde Kill," which crossed Chatham Street near Roosevelt Street, and came out into the East River at the bottom of James Street. This "Kill" or small stream was then and long afterwards regarded as the boundary line between the city and the country, and is distinguished as such in many of the early municipal regulations. (38).

It crossed the only road leading from the City, and being a convenient line of separation, the land below it, that is, between it and the City Wall, or the present Wall Street, was uniformly known as the "City Commons," (39) and all above and beyond it upon this road was "outside the City." This little stream was also the southern boundary of a farm which extended along what is now Chatham Street, to a little above Oliver Street, from whence the line of this farm ran to about the present Madison Street, and then southerly along Madison Street to the Kill, or small stream mentioned. This farm was one of the original "Bouweries," granted in 1650, by Governor Stuyvesant to Wolfert Webbers. The space between it and the East River was in part a meadow and in part a low marshy ground, or swamp. The elevated land above was known in the Dutch period as Wolfert's Bouwery; and the land below as Wolfert's Meadow. Near the point where this farm began, on the highway, or a little below the present corner of Chatham and Roosevelt Streets, there was a copious spring of pure and delightful water, that descended

---

38. Val. Man. for 1866, pp. 611.
39. Ordinances of Nov. 18th 1731, 20th, 27th, 33d.

from and was filtered through the range of hills above. There was at this period and for a long time afterwards, no city perhaps in the world, the water of which was as bad as that of New York. It was, in fact, so bad that horses coming in from the country wouldn't drink it. This spring was therefore highly prized, and was a notable place with which all the inhabitants of the City were familiar, and to which all classes were accustomed to resort, especially on Sundays. and holidays, for the pleasure of drinking this water. Both it and the kill or stream were known in 1728, and long before and afterwards as the "Fresh Water," (40) and the statement in the petition of the Jewish inhabitants in 1728 that they had "some years since purchased a small piece of land beyond the Fresh Water, for a burying place," indicates that this burying ground was beyond and very near this well-known spring.

The spring was situated in a low valley, close to the highway and to the kill, which at this point (Chatham near Roosevelt Street) was crossed by a bridge called the Kissing Bridge, from an old custom of the city, by which any gentleman riding or walking across this bridge with a lady had the right to salute her. The land above rose as it does now, until it reached its general level above the head of Chatham Square, which was then, as it is still, an open triangular space. At the broad end of this open space, between what is now Division Street and East Broadway, was the farm-house of Harmanus Rutgers, with its buildings and gardens. On the eastern side of what is now Chatham Square, near the present Oliver Street, stood a wind-mill, and to the south of this wind-mill, on the crest of the hill and facing the East, was this old Jew-

---

40. Com. Council, Minutes of May 19th, 1732.

ish burial ground. It is indicated upon the earliest map known of the city, that of 1664, and its exact place is easily determined by Holland's map of 1757, Maerschalckm's of 1755, and 1763, Ratzer's of 1765, and Montresor's of 1775. It was in 1728, and for many years afterwards, in a very beautiful position overlooking the meadows below and the city to the south of it and commanding an extensive view of the course of the East River and of the neighboring shores of Long Island. (41).

It is said in Booth's History of the City of New York, that a Jewish cemetery was first established in the city in 1731, that it was bounded by Chatham, Oliver, Henry and Catherine Streets, and was given by Noe Willey, of London, to his three sons, merchants in New York, to be held as a burial place for the Jewish nation forever. No part of this statement is correct. Roy, not Noe Willey, an apothecary of London, became the owner of the farm or Bouwerie on which this first burying ground stood, under these circumstances. It had passed from the original proprietor, Wolfert Webbers, by successive conveyance, until it was conveyed in 1698, by William Merritt, a former Mayor of the city, to William Janeway, a purser of a British vessel of war. Janeway, in 1699, executed a mortgage upon it to Tennis and Jacob Dekay, two persons in New York, for £500, and then mortgaged it again in London, in 1700, to Roy Willey for £340, concealing the fact of the first

---

41. There is a print in Valentine's Manual for 1861. p. 520 purporting to give a view of this locality and its surroundings at an early period, with the Jewish burial ground in the distance, but like many of the prints in these manuals, it is not the copy of an actual drawing, but an imaginary production, of little value to an investigator. As a representation of the Jewish burial ground at any period, it is wholly unreliable.

mortgage. Janeway died in 1726, and Willey's mortgage being long past due, he instructed an attorney in New York to obtain the payment of it, when the existence of the first mortgage came to light. Willey then sent out a power of attorney to one Richard Davis, the surgeon of a vessel of war upon the New York station, authorizing him to do whatever might be essential to secure Willey's rights. By an act passed in the reign of William and Mary, it was declared that, if any one should join in a second mortgage upon land, concealing the existence of a prior mortgage, he should forfeit thereafter all right to redeem the land One of the Dekays was then dead, and had left his interest in the first mortgage to his widow, and Davis commenced proceedings to enable Willey, by paying the first mortgage, to cut off all claims of the Dekays, or of the heirs to Janeway, and obtain the land himself in satisfaction of his mortgage. This litigation was pending in the Court of Chancery in 1728, and this was the difficulty to which the Jewish petitioners to the Common Council, in 1728, referred, when they stated in their petition, that "they would have purchased some more land adjoining the burial-ground they then had, but it being in dispute they could not obtain any title to it." In 1729, however, a settlement was effected by Davis.

Jacob Dekay and the widow of his brother, and also the heirs of Janeway, executed conveyances to Willey, by which, without any further litigation, he became the owner of the land (42) in all of which conveyances, two places upon the farm, "the Jews' burial ground," and "the family vault of Wm. De

---

(42) N. Y. Reg of Deeds, Lib. 31, pp. 109, 406. Albany Deeds, No 9, p. 474.

Meyer," a former owner of the farm, were excepted. Roy Willey, thus having become the owner of the property, the difficulty of obtaining land adjoining the old burial place was removed, and measures were immediately taken to procure it by purchase from Willey.

Indeed, in anticipation of this settlement, Willey sent out in 1728, a power of attorney to Davis, giving him authority to execute a deed of the lands required and on the 17th of December, 1729, Davis, as the attorney of Willey, conveyed to Luis Gomez, and his three sons, Mordecai, Daniel and David, for the consideration of £30, a piece of ground which in the language of the deed, began "at the south-east corner of the Jewish burial-place," and extended to the "Highway," the present line of Chatham Square. It was an oblong piece of land, 392 feet long by 56 feet broad in the widest part, the boundaries being so arranged, and so expressed in the deed, as to take in in the rear, or southernmost part of it, the existing Jewish burial ground which as thus included, constituted about one third of the whole. (43)

This deed fixes the exact locality of the burial-ground referred to by the Jewish residents, in their

---

(43) The official papers above referred to are at present to be found in the Register's Office, New York City. Copies of them appeared in the *Menorah*, July, 1892. About 1850, some years after the land in question had ceased to be used as a burial ground, the property in question became the subject of a law-suit. The widow of one of the descendants of the original grantees sued the Tradesmen's Bank, which then owned the property, for dower, but lost the suit, because her husband's ancestors and his associates only took the land as a trust. Much interesting information in regard to the plaintiff's family and the early history of the cemetery developed in the course of the trial. See the report of the case Gomez versus Tradesmen's Bank, 4 Sandford's Reports, 102.—EDITOR.

petition to the Common Council in the previous year, and as they state in that petition that it was then full, and as the Jewish population of the city up to that time was a very small one, there can be no doubt that it was the original burial ground of 1656.

In Maerschalckm's map of 1755, sixteen years after the purchase of the additional ground from Willey, the old burial ground as it was then enclosed and fenced in, is represented as situated a little above Madison Street, and as extending over the present Oliver Street, for about one-third of the block (44) and in Lieut. Ratzer's map of 1763, (45) it is represented as still enclosed and separated from the rest of the ground, with a small square enclosure in the front of it, that I take to be the family vault of De Meyer, which had been reserved by the De Meyers when they conveyed the land, and being reserved also in the conveyance by the De Kays to Willey in 1729, could not be disturbed. (46)

On the 24th of November, 1730, Luis Gomez and his three sons, Mordecai, Daniel and David, executed an instrument reciting the conveyance of the lands by David to them as the agent of Willey; that they had appropriated £30 for the purchase of it "for a burial

---

(44) Val. Man. for 1849, p. 140.
(45) N. Y. Reg. of Deeds, Lib. 18, pp. 166, 167. Albany Deeds, No. 9, p. 474.
(46) It is said in Scovill's Old Merchants of New York, Vol. 2. p. 121, that there were monuments upon this ground, bearing date 1652, which would be two years after the original grant of the land by Governor Stuyvesant. This date, 1652, is probably a mistake. Scovill, the author of this work, being a loose and very inaccurate writer. Greenleaf, however, the author of an account of the churches of New York, a careful and accurate writer, states that there were tombstones there of the date of 1678, a fact strengthening the conclusion that this was the first burial ground.

place for the use of the Jewish nation in general," and that the title, though in their names, was in trust; by which instrument they bound themselves in the sum of £1,000 to Jacob Franks and Nathan Levy, merchants of New York, that they would not sell the land or any part of it, but that it should remain "forever" thereafter as "a burying place for the Jewish nation in general and to no other use whatever." (47)

This enlargement of the original burying ground having been thus affected, the two lots in Gold Street were not used for the purpose for which they were bought, but remained in the Gomez family, as I find they were advertised for sale by the widow of Mordecai Gomez in 1752. (48)

·When Madison, then called Baucker Street, was laid out in 1755, the rear of the burial ground was extended to that street, and when the upper part of Oliver Street, then called Fayette Street, was opened after the Revolution, it took off a part of the burial ground extending over Oliver Street, and when Chatham Square was regulated and paved about the commencement of this century, it took off a portion of the front. In this condition it remained with but few material alterations until 1823, when the Congregation Shearith Israel, the Mill Street Synagogue, applied to Chancellor Kent for liberty to sell the part fronting on Chatham Square, 45 feet to the depth of 88 feet, which was granted, and it was accordingly sold to the Tradesmen's Bank for $15,000, but how or in what way this Congregation obtained or could convey any title to it, does not appear. Daniel Gomez, the survivor of the four original trus-

---

(47) N. Y. Reg. of Deeds, Lib. 31, p. 374.
(48) N. Y. Gazette, Feb. 3d, 1752.

tees, removed before the Revolution to Philadelphia, and, 1828 his grandson, Isaac Gomez, Jr., released to the Mill Street Synagogue all his estate or right in the land, as the surviving representative of his grandfather, David Gomez, and a few days after this release was executed, this Congregation applied to Chancellor Walworth for liberty to sell the rear part of the land, fronting upon Oliver and Madison Streets. There was at that time a heavy assessment on it of $11,626.54, for the improvements made in the vicinity, whilst it was no longer available as a burial ground, the City Corporation having prohibited burials in that part of the city. The Congregation Shearith Israel, to prevent its being sold for the payment of the assessment, mortgaged it to Harman Hendricks, who had advanced the money to pay the assessment and the accumulated interest, and the Congregation having incurred an additional debt to enable them to purchase a new burial ground in Eleventh Street, this application to the Court of Chancery was made that they might pay off the whole debt, $22,132.43, by the sale of the rear part of the ground. The application was granted, and the portion referred to was sold in 1829 to David Bryson and Robert Swanton. Finally, a few years ago, the Bowery was extended through what remained of it, and all that is now left is the small enclosure fronting the New Bowery, before referred to, a portion of which is a part of the original burying ground of 1656.

On the 15th of November, 1727, an act was passed by the General Assembly of New York providing that, when the oath of abjuration was to be taken by any one of his Majesty's subjects professing the Jewish religion, the words "upon the true faith of a Christian," might be omitted, and on the 18th of the same month an act was passed naturalizing Daniel

Nunez Da Costa, a Jewish resident of the city of New York, (49) which was virtually abrogating the general act of 1683, before referred to, which limited the naturalization of foreigners to those professing the Christian religion. (50).

In 1737, the election of Col. Frederick Phillips as a representative to the General Assembly for the County of Westchester was contested by Capt. Cornelius Van Horne, who claimed the seat. The Assembly ordered an investigation before the House, and after Van Horne's case had been heard, Col. Phillips called some persons of the Jewish persuasion to give evidence on behalf of Phillips, when an objection was made to their competency as witnesses. The matter was argued by the counsel for the respective parties, and Col. Phillips desiring that the sense of the House should be taken, both parties were requested to withdraw, and after some time they were called in and informed by the Speaker that it was the opinion of the House that "none of the Jewish profession could be admitted as evidence" in such a controversy. From what subsequently occurred, it would seem that some of those who had voted at this election were Jews, for, after again hear-

---

49. Strangely enough, some years before this statute was passed, in July, 1723, an act was passed naturalizing the following among others: Abraham Isaacs, David Elias, Jacob Hays, Joseph Simson, Isaac Rodrigues, Solomon Myers. It does not appear that any special provision, permitting them to omit the words "upon the true faith of a Christian." was included in the act. (Journal of Legislative Council of New York, Vol. I, p. 127.) The reader is referred to a lengthy consideration of the various statutes of naturalization, contained in a letter written by Judge Daly some years ago, and reprinted in "The Jewish Messenger." See Appendix II.—EDITOR.

50. Journal of Legislative Council of New York, Vol. I, xii. pp. 560, 561.

ing arguments from the counsel of both parties, the House resolved that, as it did not appear that persons of the Jewish religion had a right to vote for members of Parliament in Great Britain, it was the unanimous opinion of the House that they could not be admitted to vote for representatives in the colony (51). The author of the continuation of Smith's History of New York refers to this as a remarkable decision, and in explanation of it says: "that Catholics and Jews had long been peculiarly obnoxious to the colonists," that "the first settlers being Dutch, and mostly of the Reformed Protestant religion, and the migrations from England, since the colony belonged to the Crown, being principally Episcopal, both united in their aversion to the Catholics and Jews." (52) But there is no ground for inferring that this decision proceeded from any peculiar colonial aversion to the Jews. The question was simply one of law. The counsels of the respective contestants availed themselves as is usual in such cases, of every legal objection that would operate to the advantage of their case, and this point being raised, the House had to pass upon it. (53) The law of the Colony of New York

51. N. Y. Journal of Assembly, Vol. I., p 712, printed by H. Saines, 1764.

52. Smith's History of New York, Albany edition, of 1814, p. 423.

53. As this was a contested election case, it can scarcely be possible that the arguments advanced on behalf of the one side would have secured a unanimous vote in their favor, had they not been convincing. It is, however, another question whether any one specially espousing the cause of the Jews and acquainted with everything bearing on the subject was present, to present the contrary view. There is no record of any such plea or pleader. As stated elsewhere, however, the legal question involved is by no means so one-sided as appears from the above; the reasons for my opinion will be found elsewhere. Upon this particular resolution, the following criticism is found in the writings of Wm H.

was especially modeled upon that of the mother country. Unlike the New England colonies, New York was a conquered province and when it was taken from the Dutch, the English mode of procedure in all matters of law and government, was introduced bodily, and from this circumstance English forms, precedents, and modes of proceedings came into use to an extent that did not prevail in other colonies where the people themselves had been left to originate and frame such a system of government and laws as was suggested by their wants and was most conducive to their interests. When the legislative Assembly of New York, therefore, unanimously decided that no Jew could vote for a member of that body, they were but simply declaring the law as it existed in England, for it was not until a comparatively recent period that a Jew could vote at an election in Great Britain (54).

Seward, immediately following strong commendation of this very legislature: "Yet the record contains one spot which the friends of rational liberty would wish to see effaced. On a question concerning a contested seat, the Assembly resolved that Jews could neither vote for representatives nor be admitted as witnesses."
—EDITOR.

54. Appendix II. contains a very valuable exposition of the Legal Status of the Jews in England, and it is clear from an examination of the Journal of the Legislative Council of New York, that they limited their consideration of the question to an inquiry as to the legal status of the Jews of England,and adapted the same standard. Judge Daly's exposition of this is unassailable.

I wish, however, to offer a brief for the Jews, and shall proceed to a consideration of some of the colonial laws bearing on the subject. Before doing so, I wish to call attention to the fact that this very session of the Legislature was conspicuous for its championship of colonial liberty and charter rights over against British royalistic expositions of them.

We have seen that in the Dutch period orders were issued on April 21, 1657, by the Director General and Council, requiring the

There was, as the writer suggests, a very strong antipathy to Jews and Roman Catholics. Indeed, so intolerant was their spirit in respect to them, that there were few of any of those persuasions at that time in the colony. But the feeling in respect to the Jews was constantly relaxing, as will appear from what has been already narrated. They were comparatively a small body, dwelling chiefly in the City of New York, and so far from being regarded with aversion they enjoyed privileges not extended to Jews in other colonies, and had among their number some of the most influential and respected merchants of the city. Smith, who was much better able to judge than the writer, who continued his history, in speaking of the Jews, says that, "they were not inconsiderable for their numbers;" but there is contemporary evidence which is decisive. Kalm, the Swedish traveler, visited New York eight years after the period of which I am writing, and remained in the city and in the colony a sufficient length of time to render all that he has written exceedingly valuable. He says, "There are many Jews settled in New York who possess great privileges. They have a synagogue and houses, great country-seats of their own property, and are allowed to keep shops in the town. They have likewise several ships which they freight and send out with their goods."

Burgomasters of New Amsterdam to admit Salvator D'Andrada and other Jews, petitioners, to the rights of citizenship. Under the Dutch, the Jews had freedom of trade and the privilege of admission into the trade guilds, and their worship in private quarters was not interfered with. By the express terms of the Capitulation of New Amsterdam, it was agreed by the British that "All people in New Amsterdam shall still continue free denizens and shall enjoy their lands, houses, goods, whatsoever, etc.," and also that " The Dutch here shall enjoy the liberty of their consciences in

In fine, the Jews enjoy all the privileges common to
the other inhabitants of this town and province" (55)

Divine worship and Church discipline." The Jews residing
within the city came within the letter and the spirit of these stipu‑
lations, which were reiterated in the Treaty of Brida.

We have already referred to various Jews who became freemen
of New York, under the provisions of the ducal or royal charters of
New York. In addition to those I have named elsewhere, I may
add Joshua David, Sr. and Jr., Moses Levy, Isaac Rodrigues
Marques, Joseph Isaacs Butcher, and others, who were admitted
prior to 1700, and thus secured trade privileges and the right to
vote for officers. (See N. Y. Hist. Society Collections for 1885.)

Strangely enough, the Statute of New York, George I., passed
in 1715, which provided for the mode of naturalizing aliens subse‑
quent to its enactment in Section 4, expressly limits the privilege
to Protestants, but by a former section of the same statute "every
person of foreign birth now alive, and who did inhabit within the
Colony before the said first day of November, 1683, shall forever
hereafter be deemed to have been naturalized, and shall enjoy all
the Rights, Privileges and Advantages that any of his Majesty's
natural-born subjects of this Colony do or of right ought to enjoy."
(Laws of New York, 1691, 1773, p. 99.) This section contains
no such limitation as to Religion, and must have had the effect
of naturalizing Jewish residents, who had lived in the State prior
to 1683.

After this period, 1723-1727, etc., as stated in the text and in
Note 49, Jews were naturalized by special act. Taking into con‑
sideration, therefore, these colonial laws and statutes, as well as
the international obligations created by the capitulation of 1664,
and the Treaty of Brida, I think that the Legislature should have
reached a contrary result in the election controversy of 1737. With
the effects of the English statutes of 13 Geo. II. c. 7, I shall not
deal as Judge Daly has referred to it at length. Attorney-General
Rosendale of this State pointed out at the recent meeting of the
American Jewish Historical Society, that this Act provided for
keeping a registry of the names of all aliens naturalized under it in
England, and that the lists might be still accessible in England,
and prove of considerable value in identifying American Jewish
settlers.—EDITOR.

55. This reference to the Jews of New York is of considerable
interest; I give it in full, therefore:

This is very conclusive, and he had the means of obtaining correct information, for he says that during his residence in the city he was frequently in company with Jews, and that he went twice to the synagogue in Mill

"Nov. 2 (1748). Besides the different sects of Christians, there are many Jews settled in New York, who possess great privileges. They have a synagogue and houses, and great country-seats of their own property, and are allowed to keep shops in town. They have likewise several ships, which they freight, and send out with their own goods. In fine they enjoy all the privileges common to the other inhabitants of this town and province.

During my residence at New York this time and in the next two years, I was frequently in company with Jews. I was informed, among other things, that these people never boiled any meat for themselves on Saturday, but that they always did it the day before; and that in winter they kept no fire during the whole Saturday. They commonly eat no pork; yet I have been told by several men of credit, that many of them (especially among the young Jews) when traveling, did not make the least difficulty about eating this, or any other meat that was put before them; even though they were in company with Christians. I was in their synagogue last evening for the first time, and this day at noon visited it again, and each time I was put into a particular seat which was set apart for strangers or Christians. A young Rabbi read the Divine service; which was partly in Hebrew and partly in the Rabbinical dialect. Both men and women were dressed entirely in the English fashion; the former had all of them their hats on, and did not once take them off during service. The galleries, I observed, were appropriated to the ladies, while the men sat below. During prayers, the men spread a white cloth over their heads, which perhaps is to represent sackcloth. But I observed that the wealthier sort of people had a much richer sort of cloth than the poorer ones. Many of the men had Hebrew books, in which they sang and read alternately. The Rabbi stood in the middle of the synagogue, and read with his face turned towards the east; he spoke, however, so fast as to make it almost impossible for any one to understand what he said."—Travels in North America, by Peter Kalm, reprinted in Pinkerton's Voyages and Travels Vol. XII. p. 455-6. This description of New York City was reprinted in the Manual of the Common Council of New York for 1869, p. 837 at pp. 841-2.—EDITOR.

Street to witness their religious exercises. It may be inferred from this statement that they enjoyed at this time every civil and political privilege, except the right to vote for members of the colonial Legislature, which was withheld, not in any spirit of local prejudice, but in conformity to what had been the rule in Great Britain for centuries, and which was regarded as controlling in the colonies.

There is but little to say respecting the further history of the Jews in the Colony of New York, after the period to which I have last referred, 1748 (56).

An outrage perpetrated upon the rights of one of them in 1749, which was made the subject of an official communication by Governor Clinton, may be referred to as illustrating the difficulty at that time in the colony, of obtaining justice when the perpetrator belonged to one of the influential aristocratic families. A Jew from Holland, where, according to the record, "he had lived in a handsome manner, and had kept his own coach, but had become unfortunate" emigrated to New York with his wife, who in personal appearance resembled Lady Clinton, the wife of the Governor, a dignified and fine-looking woman. Oliver De Lancey, the brother of the Chief Justice of the Province, with several associates, having disguised their persons and blackened their faces, went to this man's residence and after breaking his windows and forcing open his door, entered his dwelling, "where they pulled and tossed everything to pieces," during which De Lancey proffered in an indecent speech to take improper liberties with the man's wife, for the reason, as he averred, that she

---

56. The further account of the Jews in New York up to Note 60 inclusive appeared several years later in "The Jewish Times," December 3, 1875. For convenience, I have incorporated it here.—EDITOR.

was like Lady Clinton. The insulted husband, whose privacy and dwelling had thus been invaded, applied to the three leading lawyers of the province to institute proceedings against the offenders, and received from each the same answer, that it was impossible to do anything, as the principal offender was a brother of the Chief Justice (57).

From this period to the American Revolution, there was but little increase in the Jewish population. During the quarter of a century that preceded that event, the population of New York increased at a greater ratio than at any previous period. It took half a century—from 1700-1750—for it to double; but it more than doubled in the twenty-five years that followed, increasing from about 9000 in 1750, to about 23,000 in 1776. The Jewish population, however, did not augment in the same proportion. It received some additions by emigration, chiefly from England, but not sufficient to counteract the loss of others who went to Newport, Charleston or Philadelphia.

Though small, however, it still continued to be a highly respectable and influential body, having among its members some of the principal merchants of the city. Of this number was Hayman Levy, who was the head of one of the principal mercantile firms of the city, Levy, Lyons & Co., having a branch in Europe, Levy, Solomon & Co. Mr. Levy carried on an extensive business for many years, chiefly among the Indians, by whom he was widely known and with

---

57. Governor Clinton's letter, is to be found in Colonial Documents Relating to the State of New York, Vol. VI. p. 471. From the same it appears that the culprit, Oliver De Lancey, was guilty of other riotous proceedings, and there is nothing to show that the failure to secure his punishment was in any way due to the fact that the injured parties were Jews.—EDITOR.

whom he had great influence. His place of business was in Mill Street, not far from the synagogue, and as he not only purchased all that the Indians brought for traffic, but kept everything in his large establishment to supply their wants, the Indians who came to the city dealt largely with him, and at certain seasons of the year were to be seen in large numbers lining the street in the vicinity of his warehouse.

The great respect they entertained for him and the universal confidence they had in him, were due to his thorough knowledge of their character, habits and wants, and to the fact that he was, in all his relations with them, and with others, an honest and high-minded merchant. From his extensive connection with them, he became the largest fur trader in the colonies and one of the most opulent merchants in the city.

The restrictive acts of Parliament, however, and the general colonial policy pursued by the government, produced an injurious effect upon the commerce and industrial interest of New York, and Hayman Levy, from his widely extended business was among the first to feel it. He failed in 1768, but so productive was his estate and so well had his business been conducted, that his assignees were enabled to discharge the whole of his indebtedness, with interest. All his property was destroyed by the great fire in 1776, but notwithstanding this additional calamity he was enabled to carry on business afterwards on his own account until his death in 1790.

Upon his books are entries of monies paid to John Jacob Astor, for beating furs, at the rate of one dollar a day. As Mr. Astor, the founder of the colossal fortune now inherited by his heirs, came to New York in 1784 and began business on his own account in 1786, Hayman Levy was probably one of the first persons by whom he was employed. In 1779, a daughter of this prominent merchant, Miss Zeporah Levy, who has been described as a beautiful woman, was married to Benjamin Hendricks, a native of this city, the founder of a well-known, long maintained and wealthy commercial house. Mrs. Hendricks survived to 1833, leaving behind her seventy grandchildren.

Another prominent Israelite merchant and shipowner of this period was Sampson Simson. He has been described as a man of great liberality, humanity, and of the strictest integrity, sincere and unpretending in his religious convictions. He took an active part among the patriotic merchants who resisted the aggressive acts of the British Government, and died in 1775.

Isaac Gomez was also a well-known Jewish merchant of that time. I am unable to say whether he belonged to the family of that name previously referred to, or whether he was the progenitor, or connected with Abraham and Benjamin Gomez, the principals of a leading Jewish commercial house in the first part of the present century.(58.)

---

58. It is interesting to note in this connection an incident to which Prof. Cyrus Adler recently called attention; his information was based on an unpublished letter of Jared Sparks. "At the outbreak of the Revolutionary War a Mr. Gomez of New York proposed to a member of the Continental Congress that he form a company of soldiers for service. The member of Congress remonstrated with Mr. Gomez on the score of age, he then being 68, to which Mr. Gomez replied that he could stop a bullet as well as a younger man." Report of Organization American Jewish Historical Society, p. 11. A number of other references to the service of Jews in the American army during the Revolution and the later Wars are at hand, but it would lead us too far from our subject to give them here. Hon. Simon Wolf will soon offer us the fruits of

It would exceed the limits I have proposed to myself, to give an account of the Israelites who have been especially prominent in New York after the Revolution; I will however, mention one, as he was the father of one of your most distinguished members, Emanuel B. Hart. Bernard Hart was born in England in 1764. He came to this country in 1777, and after a short residence in Canada, settled in the City of New York in 1780. In the early part of his career, he carried on some commercial transactions with Canada, and was an insurance broker until about 1802, when he became one of the members of the large auction and commission house of Lispenard and Hart. In 1806, he married a daughter of Benjamin Seixas, a leading Jewish merchant of the city, the lady being one of eight sisters, all of whom are said by a writer who knew them to have been remarkable for "their wonderful beauty and exceeding loveliness, both in person and character." (59) This writer, Joseph A. Scovill, who had been himself a merchant, speaks of Mr. Hart, in view of his social influences, commercial position, and active humanity, as "towering aloft among the magnates of the city of the last and present century." He describes him during the prevalence of the Yellow Fever in New York, in 1795, as unceasing in his exertions night and day, among the sick and dying; hardly giving himself time to sleep or eat, in his unremitting efforts for the relief of the suffering, and being—to employ the language of the writer —an angel of mercy in the awful days of that great pestilence.

---

his labors in this direction. As for the New York Jews, it speaks well for their patriotism that so many should have migrated to Philadelphia just before the British occupation of New York City. Many returned to New York subsequently.—EDITOR.

59. Scovill's "Old Merchants" of New York, Vol. II. p, 125.

He was the founder and chief officer of a well-known social institution of the period, called "The Friary," the parent of our present Clubs, and a prominent member of several other organizations, of different names, composed chiefly of merchants, who met in the evening at some leading tavern for the purpose of intercourse, and to discuss business matters, a kind of social and commercial exchange. Upon the formation of the Board of Brokers about 1818, he became the Secretary of that body, which position he held for the remainder of his life, dying in the city in 1855, at the advanced age of 91.

Mr. Scovill, in referring to the small number of Jewish merchants in this city in the early part of the present century, and the great contrast, at the period at which he was writing (1868), concludes with this remark: "There are now," he says, "80,000 Israelites in this city, and it is the high standard of excellence of the Old Israelite Merchants of 1800, that has made the race occupy the proud position it now holds in this city and in the nation."

About the middle of the last century, but in what year I am not able to state, the Rev. Joseph Isaac Jerushalem Pinto became the minister of the synagogue in Mill Street. He died in 1763, and in 1766 was succeeded by the Rev. Gershom Seixas, who continued in charge of the congregation for the long period of 50 years. Mr. Seixas was a man much esteemed not only among his own people, but in the community generally. He was a Trustee of Columbia College, from 1787 to 1815, when he resigned, an indication of the respect entertained for him, as the government of Columbia College has, from its foundation, been confided almost exclusively to Episcopalians. He died in 1816, and was succeeded by Rev. Moses L. M. Peixotto. The synagogue erected in 1728, being decayed, was torn down in 1818, and a new stone edifice, 33 by 58 feet, was erected upon the same site(60). It was a plain, unostentatious building, provided in the interior with a gallery for females.

Mr. Peixotto, when placed in charge of the congregation, was a merchant in Front Street, and continued to follow his mercantile calling for two years afterwards. In 1820, he withdrew altogether from business, taking up his residence at 105 Greenwich Street, from which he removed in 1822 to 15 Mill Street, next to the synagogue, where he died in 1827. He was a learned man, thoroughly versed in Hebrew, and a master of several other languages. I remember him as a dark-featured, square-built, middle-sized man, greatly addicted to snuff-taking, who spoke English with a strong accent, and somewhat imperfectly. His successor was the Rev. Isaac B. Seixas, a nephew of the former incumbent of that name, a gentleman very much esteemed, who remained in his charge until his death, in 1839, when he was succeeded by the Rev. Jacques J. Lyons.

In 1824, a portion of the congregation, consisting mainly of members of Polish or German birth, separated from the synagogue in Mill Street, and purchasing a church in Elm Street, formed a distinct congregation under the Rev. Mr. Hart, who was succeeded by the Rev. Mr. Meyer, and in 1839, by the Rev. S. M. Isaacs. In 1844, Mr. Isaacs, with a portion of the members withdrew, and formed a new congregation in Franklin Street, and constituted, with Mr. Isaacs their minister, the synagogue now in 44th Street.

In 1833, the congregation in Mill Street sold the church property there, and erected a new synagogue

---

60) Hardie's N. Y. p. 163.

in Crosby Street, near Spring Street, which they also afterwards, sold and erected the fine synagogue they now occupy in 19th Street. As the denomination have since greatly multiplied in New York, it would involve too much detail to give an account of the subsequent congregations. It will suffice to say that the Jews have now (1872) in New York 29 synagogues, and as a proportional part of the population, they are now estimated at about 70,000. (61)

PENNSYLVANIA.

My information is very meagre respecting the early settlement of the Jews in Pennsylvania. Several prominent families were established at Philadelphia, in the middle of the last century, some of whom were connected with those in New York (62). The Jews, both of Philadelphia and of New York, with few, if any, exceptions, were warm adherents of the American Revolution. Prominent over all others, of the Jewish persuasion, was Haym Salomon. He was a native of Poland. When he came to this country, I do not know, nor do I know anything respecting him, until about the breaking out of the Revolution, when he was a man of large private fortune, engaged in commercial pursuits, of great financial resources, and ability, and of the highest personal integrity. He espoused the cause of the colonists, with great ardor, and supplied the government from his own means

---

61) In the Supplementary Chapter written by Judge Daly, for this series, the subject is continued. Even before 1833, other Jewish congregations existed in New York City besides those named.—EDITOR.

62) At the recent meeting of the Jewish Historical Society, held in Philadelphia, several interesting and very elaborate papers on the early history of the Jews in Philadelphia were read. No doubt the proceedings of the Society, the first volume of which is soon to appear, will cast much new light on the subject.—EDITOR.

with a large amount of money, at the most critical periods of the struggle. As appeared from documentary evidence, afterwards submitted to Congress, he advanced to the Government altogether $658,007.13, an enormous sum at that period for a private individual, when all commerce and busines was prostrated. But in addition to this, he supplied delegates to Congress and officers of the army and of the government with the means of defraying their ordinary expenses; among whom were Jefferson, Madison, Lee, Steuben, Mifflin, St. Clair, Wilson, Monroe, and Mercer. Madison wrote to the authorities in Virginia in 1783, "I am fast relapsing into pecuniary distress, and the case of my brethren is especially alarming. I have been a pensioner, for some time, upon the bounty of Haym Salomon. I am almost ashamed to reiterate my wants so incessantly to you. The kindness of Haym Salomon is a fund that will preserve me from extremities, but I never resort to it without great mortification, as he obstinately rejects all recompense."

Such was the condition of many of our public men, at this period, that Robert Morris, writing in 1783, said that many of them could not, without payment, perform their duties, and must have gone to jail for the debts they had contracted to enable them to live, had they not received private assistance; and Robert Morris himself, in 1805, became an inmate of a debtor's jail, through the responsibilities he had assumed, and the losses he had sustained in his efforts as its chief financial officer to sustain the government. Mr. Salomon was taken prisoner as early as 1775, and being confined at New York in that lonesome prison, the Provost, he contracted a disease which caused his death towards the close of the war. He died before he had taken any steps to secure a reimbursement by the Government of the large amount he had loaned it, and left a wife and four small children, to use the language of a Congressional report, "to hazard and neglect." Applications have been made to Congress by his heirs for the repayment of the amount loaned, or at least for some part of it. These applications led to the most thorough searches in the archives of the Government, and among the papers of Robert Morris, but nothing was found showing that any portion of the amount had ever been repaid. Madison, in 1827, urged that the memorialists might be indemnified; and reports in their favor have frequently been made by Congressional committees, but down to 1864, not a dollar has been paid to them, a fact, I regret to say, which affords support to the oft-repeated observations of the ingratitude of republics. (63)

In 1782, the synagogue Mickve Israel was erected in Philadelphia, in Cherry Street, between Third and Fourth Streets. It appears from the Pennsylvania Archives (64), that a formal invitation was extended to the President and other officers of Pennsylvania to be present at the consecration of it, and that the Trustees were Jonas Phillips, President; Michael Gratz, Solomon Marache, Solomon M. Cohen, and Simon Nathan. It appears to have been the first synagogue erected in that city, from which I infer that the Jews residents there before that period must have been very few in number. In 1824, it was replaced by a more spacious and elegant structure. In 1825, there were two synagogues, and in 1854, five.

Michael Gratz, one of the trustees above-named,

---

63. Hon. Simon Wolf has very recently been pressing these claims before Congress, on behalf of the descendants of Haym Salomon. An extremely interesting article on Mr. Salomon's services was written by Mr Wolf, and appeared in the *Reform Advocate's* first anniversary number, February 20, 1892.—EDITOR.

64. Vol. X. p. 701, 13 Penn. Col. 367.

was the father of Rebecca Gratz, a maiden lady of Philadelphia, widely known there in all social circles, who lived to an advanced age, and distinguished not only for her stately carriage, dignified manners and personal beauty, but for her intellectual superiority and acquirements. It is said that Scott drew his character of Rebecca in "Ivanhoe" from the account he received of this interesting woman; that when Lord Jeffrey visited this country in 1814 to marry Miss Wilkes, the future Lady Jeffrey, he made the acquaintance of Miss Gratz; that he was struck with her beauty and dignified character, and gave such a glowing account of her to Scott that the great novelist embodied the description he received in the charter of Rebecca. The story is not in itself improbable, as Scott is known to have drawn several of his imaginary characters from real personages. A Philadelphia newspaper has recently published this story with Washington Irving instead of Lord Jeffrey, Irving having visited Scott about a year before the latter wrote "Ivanhoe." The writer adds that Rebecca Gratz inspired Irving with the warmest regard he ever gave to any woman; that she was the subject of his addresses at her house in Philadelphia, until she convinced him that no argument would ever induce her to forego her faith by marrying a Christian. Irving knew Miss Gratz, and Joseph Gratz, her brother or relative, was one of his early intimates, which is about all the foundation the writer had, I apprehend, for this statement. In addition, Lockhart says that the introduction of the Jewish character in "Ivanhoe" was suggested to Scott by his friend, Mr. Skene, in the early part of 1819, long after Mr. Irving's visit, whilst the great writer was suffering from severe illness; that Mr. Skene had passed some time in his youth in Germany, where he had seen much of the Jews, of whom, whilst he was attending his sick friend, he recounted many of his reminiscences ; and partly in seriousness, and partly to turn Scott's mind upon something that might divert it in his illness, Mr. Skene suggested that a group of Jews would be an interesting feature if Scott could contrive to bring them into his next novel ; that after the appearance of "Ivanhoe", Scott called Mr. Skene's attention to this conversation with the remark : "You will find this book owes not a little to your German reminiscences." (65.)

It is very probable that the name of Rebecca and the resemblance of Miss Gratz in person and character to the Jewish maiden that Scott has immortalized, was all the foundation there was for this story, which for half a century has been current in social circles in Philadelphia and New York. She seems to have been in every way worthy of Scott's ideal, for she had all Rebecca's devotion to her ancient faith, and attachment to her people, and throughout her life gave a certain portion of her time to unostentatious acts of benevolence in the relief of the wretched and suffering.

MARYLAND.

Maryland (66) has frequently been referred to as among the first of the colonies which, in the language of Bancroft, "adopted religious freedom as the basis of the State." (67.) It did, but with this

---

65. Lockhart's " Life of Scott," Vol. 6, pp. 178 and 179.
66. Much new light on the early history of the Jews in Maryland was cast by the able paper already referred to on Jacob Lombroso; read by Mr. J. H. Hollander, at the recent meeting of the American Jewish Historical Society. Hon. Oscar S. Straus has kindly called my attention to interesting data on the history of the Jews of Maryland contained in a book of speeches on the " Jew Bill," 1824, edited by Brackenridge, in his possession.
67. Bancroft's " History of the U.S.," p. 256. Langford, 27–32,

qualification : that it was limited to those within the province professing to believe in Jesus Christ, and was accompanied by a proviso which declared that any person who denied the Trinity should be *punished with death*. Maryland was, therefore, no place for Jews ; and even after the Revolution, by the bill of rights and constitution of Maryland, no one could hold any employment of profit or confidence under "the State" without signing a declaration that he believed in the Christian religion ; and this exclusion of all of the Jewish faith was retained for a long time after the War of Independence. Efforts were made in the Legislature in 1801 and 1804 to obtain the repeal of this intolerant provision, but upon each occasion more than two-thirds of the members voted against its repeal. These efforts were renewed in 1819, when a very able report was submitted by the committee to whom the subject was referred, recommending that there should be no religious test whatever, together with a bill to effect that object. The tenacity, in fact, with which Maryland adhered to this provision had been previously widely discussed over the whole country, and universally condemned in other States. John Adams, in a letter written in 1818, gave expression to the wish that "the Jews might be admitted to all the privileges of citizens of every country of the world, and that in this country, especially, we ought to annul every narrow idea in religion, government and commerce." Jefferson and Madison were equally explicit in their condemnation of this intolerant restriction, but when the bill, reported by the committee, came up in the Legislature, it was rejected, about the same proportion of members voting against it (68). In a few years afterwards,

---

68. Niles' "Register," Vol. 15, p. 388. Suppl. p. 9 13.—ED.

however, the provision was repealed, and in 1824 two gentlemen of the Jewish persuasion were elected members of the City Council of Baltimore, being the first persons of that denomination who had held office in Maryland. (69.)

GEORGIA.

The great number of persons that were confined in jails in England for debt, and the injurious effects of prison life upon their habits, manners, and prospects of future usefulness, induced General Oglethorpe to set on foot a scheme for establishing a colony in America between the Altemaha and Savannah River, to which this class and other destitute persons in Great Britian might be sent with the prospect of beginning the world anew, their passage being paid, the use of a tract of land being given to each of them for the period of ten years, and provision being made for their support for the first year. A charter was obtained, accompanied by a liberal grant of money from Parliament, a company was organized, consisting of twenty-one trustees, who were clothed with plenary power for the government of the colony, and the additional funds requisite for this very expensive undertaking were to be raised by public subscription. The scheme gave rise to a great deal of public enthusiasm, and its benevolent projector, Oglethorpe, who was one of the trustees, went out with 115 of this class of persons, to what is now the State of Georgia to found the new colony.

On the day, the 7th of July, 1733, that Oglethorpe had assembled the colonists, on the site of the present city of Savannah, for the purpose of alloting to each settler his proportion of land, and of organizing a municipal government, a vessel directly from London,

---

69. Sharf's " Chronicles of Baltimore," p. 240.

came up the Savannah River, whilst the colonists were partaking of a public dinner, given at the close of the day's proceedings, and landed forty Jewish emigrants. Their arrival was not expected, for the London company knew nothing of this emigration, until the vessels containing the emigrants, had left. The trustees of the company had commissioned three persons in London, Anthony Da Costa, Francis Salvador, and Alvarez Lopez Suasso, to obtain subscriptions. They collected a sum of money, but instead of paying it into the Bank of England, which had been selected as the place of deposit for subscriptions, they appropriated it towards sending out this body of Jewish emigrants. When the trustees had been informed of what had been done, they were very indignant and vacated the "commission," given to these gentlemen, that "the public mind might be disabused of any intention to make a Jews' colony of Georgia." They used every effort to undo what had been done. They urged Da Costa, Salvador, and Suasso, to use their endeavors to have the Jews, who had emigrated, removed from the colony, and wrote to Oglethorpe, informing him of the departure of these Jewish emigrants, "expressing the hope that they would receive no encouragement from him," and that he would "use his best endeavors to prevent their settling in Georgia, as it would be prejudicial to the trade and welfare of the colony."

In the judgment of a writer who has commented upon this proceeding (70) this course upon the part of the trustees was necessary, as the money essential to carry on the enterprise, had to be obtained by public subscriptions which would have been materially diminished, had it been understood that it was the

---

70. Steven's History of Georgia, Vol. 1, p. 102.

intention of the trustees to encourage the emigration of Jews. This was probably true, and it shows how unreasonable and deep-seated was the prejudice at that time in England against people of the Jewish persuasion, when it was supposed that the prospects of a colony, to be composed in a large degree of the inmates of jails, would have been injured if Jews were allowed to go and settle there.

General Oglethorpe was a chivalric, high-toned and benevolent man, upon whom the arrival of these Jewish emigrants had a very different effect from that it had upon his London associates. He regarded them as a valuable acquisition, and, before he received the letter of the trustees, he had dispatched a letter to them commendatory of the new emigrants, dwelling upon their good conduct and calling the attention of the trustees especially to one of their number, Dr. Nunis, for his humane attention to the sick and many other valuable services. (71). It would have been extraordinary, indeed, if he had done otherwise, for as a body they were in marked contrast with the other settlers, the majority of whom, from their previous habits and associations, were practically useless as colonists, being idle, dissolute and mutinous, and had the settlement of the colony depended upon them, it would never have been accomplished. These Jewish emigrants, on the contrary, were industrious and orderly, and had among them several men of high intelligence. (72) One of their number was the principal physician; another, Abraham De Lyon, was a horticulturist, who introduced successfully useful foreign plants, and in the cultivation of the vine labored assiduously to make Georgia a grape-growing country;

---
71. Stephens' Journal of Proceedings in Georgia, Vol I., p. 48. Stevens' History of Georgia, p. 101-104.
72. Graham's History of North America, Vol. I.

whilst another was afterwards the principal merchant of the colony, having extensive transactions with Oglethorpe and the London Company. In fact, had it not been for these Jewish emigrants, and the arrival afterwards of a congregation of Moravians, and of a small body of Highlanders from Scotland, this philanthropic scheme would have failed in its inception as the class for whose benefit it was specially intended, would neither labor effectually as agriculturists, nor could they be depended on as soldiers, to protect the colony from the Spaniards, who threatened its very existence.(73)

Oglethorpe's letter produced but little effect upon the London trustees. They expressed their acknowledgments for the kindness of the good physician, Dr. Nunis, in an especially English way, by requesting Oglethorpe to give him a proper gratuity for his medical services, and in adherence to their original resolution, instructed Oglethorpe to withhold from the Jewish residents any grants of land in the province. Oglethorpe, probably, did not comply with these instructions, for to have done so, in the language of a Georgia historian, would have been to have stripped the colony of some of the most worthy and industrious of its inhabitants.(74) But that result was in time brought about by the unwise policy of not allowing the colonists to manage their own affairs, and of attempting to govern them exclusively by the will of a London corporation. No scheme of colonization was perhaps ever undertaken with more disinterested

---

73. A more detailed account of some of the early experiences of the Jews in Georgia was contained in a paper by Col. Charles C. Jones, read before the American Jewish Historical Society. But he does not appear to have had any knowledge of the Sheftail Mss. referred to by Judge Daly at some length.—EDITOR.

74. Stevens' History of Georgia, Vol. I, p. 102.

motives, or more completely counteracted from want of knowledge or judgment in the carrying out of its details. It was, in fact, an attempt to revive in the primitive forests of America the decaying feudal system of Europe, and being impossible in the settlement of a new country, the persistent attempt to carry it out had no other effect but to retard the growth of the colony.

Information of a very reliable nature in respect to this Jewish emigration to Savannah, has been preserved in the narrative of one of the emigrants, Benjamin Sheftail, which was continued by his son, Mordecai Sheftail. This narrative contains the names of the first emigrants, (75) and the events that occurred respecting them and their successors to a period beyond the American Revolution. It appears from this narrative that the vessel in which they embarked was commanded by Beverly Robinson, that she sustained an injury in the River Thames, which involved considerable delay for repairs; that the passage out was a boisterous one, the vessel encountering successive gales, by one of which she was nearly wrecked off the coast of North Carolina, running into an inlet where she was detained several weeks. And this narrative differs from the other historical sources of information in the statement, that the vessel arrived in Savannah

---

75. Their names were as follows: Doctor Nunis, Mrs. Nunis, his mother, Daniel Nunis, Moses Nunis, Sipra Nunis, Shem Noah, their servant, Isaac Nunez Henriques, his wife, and Shem, their son; Raphael Bornal and his wife, David Olivera. Jacob Olivera, and his wife, David and Isaac, their sons, and Leah their daughter, Aaron Depivea, Benjamin Gideon, Jacob Costa, David Lopass, Depass and wife, Vene Real, Molena, David Moranda, David Cohen, his wife, Isaac, their son Abigail, Hannah and Grace, their daughters; Abraham Minis, his wife, and Leah and Esther, their daughters, Simeon Minis, the brother of Abraham, Jacob Towell, Benjamin Sheftail and wife, and Abraham Delyou.

on the 11th of July, 1733, four days *after* the assigning of the lots by Oglethorpe to the settlers. (76.)

Mr. Levi Sheftail, in whose possession the manuscript was thirty years ago, states that the writer of it, Benjamin Sheftail told his sons, Mordecai and Levi, and which they frequently repeated to their descendants, that the Jewish emigrants of 1733 paid their passage and laid in "all necessary supplies for the voyage, so that they were in no wise dependent on the favor or charity of the British crown for one dollar to facilitate their emigration." This can scarcely be correct in view of what occurred in London after their departure. Some of them may have done so, and Benjamin Sheftail may have been one of that number. The truth probably was, as he stated, that they were in no wise dependent upon the charity of the British crown, for the reason that the money, to facilitate the emigration of the whole body, was raised by subscription, among their co-religionists, by the three persons before named.

Previous to their departure, articles used in the ceremonial service of the synagogue were presented to them by a friend in London, and one of their first acts after their arrival was to establish a synagogue. Constituting as they did nearly one-third of the actual settlers they had a large congregation, and accordingly they rented a house on the Market Square in Savannah, for their synagogue, to which they gave the name of Mickve (assemblage) Israel, and where religious services were regularly held for some years. After the establishment of their •place of worship, other articles for the synagogue and a donation of books was sent out to them by Benjamin Mendez of London.

With the capacity and the disposition to aid mate-

---

76. *The Occident,* vol. 1. p. 379.

rially in the advancement of the colony, they had little to encourage them after the final departure of Oglethorpe. The Trustees were not only hostile to them, but the policy which this body pursued in the government of Georgia was detrimental to its progress. Placed as they were under civil disabilities, and subject with the rest of the population to the foolish restrictions imposed by this London company, many of them gradually withdrew to South Carolina, where no such restrictions existed, and settled in Charleston, attracted by the superior commercial advantage of that rising city. By the year 1742, their numbers were so diminished in Savannah, that the services in the synagogue had to be discontinued, and at last but three families of the original settlers remained : the Sheftails, Minises and De Lyons.

In about a quarter of a century, however, some of those who went to Charleston, returned Among these was Mordecai Sheftail, described as "a man of exemplary piety, who adhered closely to all the rites and ceremonies of his faith." In 1773, he gave a piece of land for a burial-ground, the mode of conveying which shows the care that was taken to prevent the land ever being applied to any other use. It was conveyed in trust to eight trustees, widely apart as follows: Abraham Hart and Joseph Gomperts of London, Sampson Simson and Joseph Simson, of New York, Isaac Hart and Jacob Riviera, of Newport, R. I., and Philip Minis and Levi Sheftail, of Savannah. It will have been observed in the previous course of this narrative, that both in this and the preceding century, the Jews are frequently referred to as a distinct people, the term commonly applied to them being "The Hebrew Nation," which on their part, it would seem, they themselves encouraged and kept up. The conveyance of this burial-ground to trustees living in three cities of this country, where their people had settled, and in London, is an indication of this feeling.

Winterbotham, who wrote what he called "An Historical and Geographical and Commercial View of the United States," a few years after its separation from Great Britain, gives a short account of the Jews in the different places in the United States, where they had settled, and in speaking of the Jews of Charleston, S. C., says: "The Jews in Charleston, among other peculiarities, in burying their dead, have these: After the funeral dirge is sung, and just before the corpse is deposited in the grave, the coffin is opened, and a small bag of earth, taken from the grave, is carefully put under the head of the deceased; then some powder, said to be earth brought *from Jerusalem, and carefully kept for this purpose*, is taken and put upon the eyes of the corpse, in token of their remembrance of the Holy Land, and of their expectations of returning thither in God's appointed time;" to which he adds: "The articles of their faith are well-known, and, therefore, need no description. They generally expect a glorious return to the Holy Land, when they shall be exalted above all the nations of the earth. And they flatter themselves that the period of their return will speedily arrive, though they do not pretend to fix the precise time." (77).

There being, again, in Savannah a sufficient number of Jews in 1774 to form a congregation, Mordecai Sheftail fitted up a room in his own house for their accommodation, where they continued to worship, their number being gradually augmented, until the breaking out of the American Revolution (78).

In that struggle the Jews of Savannah and Charles-

---

77. Winterbotham, vol. 1. p. 394.
78. *The Occident*, vol. 1, p. 487.

ton joined the Revolutionary party, and appear to have adhered to it with unwavering fidelity. Sheftail, the son of Mordecai, held some military position, and fought bravely when the Britishers were repulsed in their assault upon Savannah.

Immediately after the close of the Revolution many Israelites arrived in Savannah and made it their place of residence. Their numbers being now considerably augmented, they re-established their congregation on the 7th of July, 1786, having as their place of worship a dwelling-house, hired for the purpose. On the 30th of November, 1790, a charter was obtained, creating Levi Sheftail, Sheftail Sheftail, Cushman Polock, Joseph Abrahams, Mordecai Sheftail, Abraham Depass and Emanuel De La Motta, and their successors, a religious corporation, under the name of "The Parnass and Adjuntas of Mickva Israel of Savannah" (79).

The religious exercises of this body were conducted for many years by Dr. De La Motta, one of the incorporators, who served gratuitously, and through whose exertions a building was erected for a synagogue in 1820, upon a lot presented by the city. At its consecration a discourse was delivered by Dr. De La Motta, which attracted the attention of Thomas Jefferson and James Madison. Jefferson speaks of it as an eloquent production, which excited in him "the gratifying reflection that his own country had been the first to prove to the world two truths the most salutary to human society: that man can govern him-

---

79. The officers of the congregation of 1786 were: Phillip Minis, *Parnas;* David N. Cardoza, *Gabay;* Levi Sheftail, Cushman Polock, Joseph Abrahams, *Adjuntas;* Emanuel De La Motta, *Hazan;* and Levy Abrahams, *Secretary*. The incorporators of 1790 were Levi Sheftail, Sheftail Sheftail, Cushman Polock, Joseph Abrahams, Mordecai Sheftail, Abraham Depass and Emanuel De La Motta.—EDITOR.

self, and that religious freedom is the best array done against religious discussion." He expressed great satisfaction at the restoration of the Jews to their social rights, and coupled with a hope that has since been realized, that they would soon be found taking their position in science preparatory to doing the same in government. Madison, in referring to the discourse, says, "The history of the Jews must be forever interesting. The modern part of it is at the same time so little generally known that every light on the subject has its value. Among the features peculiar to the political system of the United States is the perfect equality of rights which it secures to every religious sect, and it is particularly pleasing to observe in the good citizenship of such as have been most distrusted and oppressed elsewhere, a happy illustration of the safety and success of this experiment of a just and beneficent policy." The synagogue was a small wooden building, exceedingly plain in its exterior, which stood alone in a broad, open space outside the city, called "The Common," but which is now a compact and populated part of Savannah. This synagogue was destroyed by fire in 1829, and was replaced by a substantial structure of brick.

I passed a portion of my youth in Savannah forty-five years ago, and at that time the Jewish residents, as a body, held a position as distinguished, if not more so, as any other class of the population. They were a recognized part of the aristocracy of the city, being, many of them, the Sheftails, the Minises and the De Lyons - direct descendants of the first settlers, the only kind of aristocracy, if it may be called such, that has ever received any recognition in this country. There was at that time, and there is still, especially in the South, an implied recognition of old families, which usually means, in the American sense, those whose ancestors came to this country either before or soon after the American Revolution, and who have at least sufficient wealth to keep up what is required in their social position. The Jews of Savannah were nearly all of this class. They had not augmented proportionately with the growth of the population, for but comparatively few of their co-religionists had come to settle in Savannah after 1799. The families were all within reasonable limits wealthy, either through inherited wealth or being engaged in pursuits in which wealth gradually is accumulated. The largest merchant, the leading lawyer and the principal physician of the city at that time were of their number, and they continued to maintain this position, for in 1843, the High Sheriff, the principal Judge of the city and the Collector of the Port, were Jews (80).

But they had a more substantial claim to the public respect. As a body, they had been uniformly distinguished for their probity, their high sense of personal honor, their courteous manners and their charity and benevolence exercised in relieving the wants of their fellow-citizens of all denominations. I recall, amid the recollections of that period, Sheftail Sheftail, Esq., the son of Mordecai and the grandson of Benjamin, the first settler, then a venerable and most striking-looking old man, habited in the garb of Franklin—a wide, spread coat, a huge cocked hat, knee breeches and large silver buckles on his shoes, who was to be seen every day in fine weather, as I have seen him, walking with a slow and stately step up and down the long piazza of his colonial-built house in Broughton Street.

The Jews who settled in Charleston were more prosperous, and their increase in numbers from

---

80. *The Occident*, vol. I, p. 250.

Europe, New York, and Newport, was much greater than in Savannah. They formed themselves into a religious society in 1750, worshiping for seven years in a small wooden house in Union near Queen Street, each year bringing an accession to their numbers. They purchased a burial ground in 1757, and removed their place of worship to a larger building in King Street; and finally in 1781, they bought a large brick edifice, which they altered into a permanent synagogue. In 1791, they were incorporated into a religious society, and at the time consisted of fifty-one families, numbering in all about 400 persons (81). In two years from this period, they had increased so rapidly that their place of worship was found to be too small, and a new and more spacious edifice was erected at a cost of $20,000, which was consecrated with imposing ceremonies in 1791. I shall not expand the account of the Jews in Charleston (82) further than to remark that the

---

81. *The Occident*, Vol, I, p. 384.

82. Much interesting information in regard to the Jews of Charleston and elsewhere derived from Mr. Isaac Harby is contained in an article in the *North American Review* for July, 1826, by S. Gilman. While the article deals chiefly with the inception of the Reform Movement among the Jews of Charleston, it gives an interesting census of the Jews of the United States and other information. He says, for instance: " In Georgia and South Carolina several Jews honorably bore arms in the Revolutionary War. My natural grandfather contributed pecuniary aid to South Carolina, and particularly to Charleston, when besieged by the British. My father-in-law was a brave grenadier in the regular American army, and fought and bled for the liberty he lived to enjoy and to hand down to his children. Numerous instances of patriotism are recorded of such Israelites." Mr. Harby estimated the number of Jews in the United States in 1826 as 6,000, divided about as follows: New England, 300–400; Pennsylvania, 300–400; New York, 950; Virginia, 400; North Carolina, 400; South Carolina, 1,200; Georgia, 400; Florida, 30 or 40; Louisiana, 100; and the remainder scattering.

In the series of articles on the Jews of Charleston, which

rapid increase of their members, immediately after the American Revolution, was owing in a great degree to the many Jews who quitted New York after that period, and settled in Charleston, as a place where their capital and industry would be more available. They brought wealth and business capacity to this southern city, where the Jews continued to be, down to the breaking out of the late Civil War, a prosperous and influential part of the business community. The Charleston Jews of the earlier period are described as exceedingly orthodox in their rigid conformity to the written and oral laws of their religion, severe penalties and forfeiture of the honors of the Synagogue being enforced by a supervisory body among them somewhat analogous to the consistorial courts in Europe. Like their brethren in Savannah, they were very charitable, devoting their time and means to relieving the sick and indigent. They organized and maintained for several years an institution, and which, for aught I know to the contrary, may still be in existence, devoted to the special purpose of relieving sick and destitute strangers in Charleston; the members of which, in the language of a Charleston writer, "visited and nursed the sick, clothed the naked and buried the dead."

The Jewish community of Newport received a valuable acquisition in the person of Aaron Lopez, who settled there about the year 1750. Possessing, a fine, safe and commodious harbor, which can be entered at all times without a pilot, and of sufficient depth for the largest vessels, Newport had great commercial

---

appeared in Vol. I. and II, of *The Occident*, and to which Judge Daly refers, the names of the earliest Jewish settlers are given as follows: Moses Cohen, Isaac De Costa, Joseph Tobias, Michael Tobias, Moses Pimenta, David de Olivera, Abraham De Costa, Mordecai Sheftail, Levy Sheftail, Michael Lazarus and Abraham Nunez Cardoza.—EDITOR.

advantages, and especially at that period, from its proximity to the New England Colonies, then the most thickly settled and industrious and active portion of North America. The advantages of this important seaport were quickly comprehended by this sagacious merchant, and to him in a larger degree than to any one else was due the rapid commercial development that followed, and which made Newport for a quarter of a century afterwards the formidable commercial rival of New York. (83) He was the means of inducing more than forty Jewish families to settle there, the heads of many of which were men of wealth, mercantile sagacity, high intelligence and enterprise. In fourteen years after Mr. Lopez settled there, Newport had 150 vessels engaged in trade with the West Indies alone, carrying on in addition an extensive whaling business, a branch to which its merchants and navigators had then been devoted for more than a century. Its West India trade was especially lucrative. Its vessels were freighted in the West Indies with molasses, which was brought to Newport, and then manufactured into rum for exportation to the coast of Africa, the vessels returning from Africa

---

83. It is with pleasure that I call attention in this connection to some remarks by the late George William Curtis, contained in an article by him on "Newport Historical and Social" (*Harper's Monthly* Vol. IX. p. 289.) The remark derives much of its force from the fact that Rhode Island was Curtis' native State whose glories he loved to dwell on, and that the story of Newport was to him "so sweet in the telling, that, like Scheherezade, beguiling the night, the chronicler would willingly while away the summer with his tale," to quote his own lines. In the article in question, he assigns three causes for the ante-revolutionary prosperity of Newport, the last of which was "the spirit of entire religious toleration, which gives to the settlement of the whole State, first at Providence and then at Newport an historical eminence no less enviable than singular. Quakers and Jews were among the earliest settlers and the most distinguished and successful of its citizens."— ED.

with slaves for the West India market. Mr. Lopez, at the breaking out of the American Revolution, was himself the owner of thirty vessels engaged in European and West India trade and the whale fisheries, and was then and for some years previously, looked upon as the most eminent and successful merchant in New England. His father-in-law, Jacob Rodriguez-Rivera, also a native of Portugal, came to Newport a few years before, about 1745, and was the first merchant there of the Jewish persuasion of any distinction ; for the Jews who settled in Newport previously were not persons of any especial prominence. (84)

Mr. Rivera was the first person who introduced the manufacture of spermaceti in America, having brought the art with him from Portugal. Acquainted with the mode of making this valuable commodity, he was naturally attached to Newport, the inhabitants of which were then actively engaged in the whale fishery, and by the introduction of the manufacture of this article he justly contributed to the prosperity of the place. He and his son-in-law, Mr. Lopez,

---

84. Peterson's History of Rhode Island, (pp. 180-181:) I have received through Charles R. Russell, Esq., of New York, the following memorandum of the names of Jews known to have been in Newport in the seventeenth century, made by N. H. Gould, Esq., of Newport, a gentleman the best informed there on the subject. Memo.: Samuel Isaac and Judah Moses, *soap boilers*; Moses and Jacob James, *workers in brass*; Isaac Benjamin, Abraham Benjamin, Isaac Moses and Jacob Frannc, or Franci, merchants and traders, how long they remained here I have no information. Jacob and Joseph Judah ; Benjamin and Moses Myers, Naphtali Myers Isaac and Nathan Lyon, David Salomon, Abraham Jacobs, Solomon Mendez, Solomon Cohen, Nathan Cohen, Aaron Cohen Isaac Cohen, and among the earliest Lodge of Freemasons were the following Israelites : Isaac Isaacs, *money broker*, Solomon Aaron Myers, Joseph Jacobs, Abraham Mendez, Eleazar Eleazar, Moses Isaacs, and Isaac Eleazar.

united in introducing this important branch of industry, and so successfully, that there were at one time no less than seventeen manufacturers of oil and candles; and Newport enjoyed the monopoly of this traffic down to the time of the breaking out of the American Revolution. Mr. Rivera resided at Newport for forty-four years. He died there in 1789, at an advanced age, and throughout his long and useful career, was distinguished for his probity and active benevolence. In his first attempt to establish himself there in business, he met with so many losses that he was obliged to compromise with his creditors, and obtain from them a release from his debts. In a very few years, having retrieved his affairs, he invited all his former creditors to dine with him, when each creditor found under his plate an order for the payment of the amount that had been released, together with interest. In addition to his integrity, he is said to have been most exemplary in the observance of all the rites, duties and obligations of his religion.

In 1763, there were between sixty and seventy Jewish families in Newport, the greater portion of whom came from Spain and Portugal, between the years 1750 and 1760. The terrible earthquake in Lisbon in 1755, which swallowed up 50,000 of the inhabitants in the short space of eight minutes, and converted that beautiful city into a mass of ruins, increased the Jewish emigration from Portugal to Newport, and what is now in Newport the north side of the Mall, was then covered with Jewish residences. They were, in fact, the chief persons of the place, for, besides Lopez and Rivera, there were many other Jewish merchants there, men of wealth, cultivation, intelligence and enterprise, and the commercial prosperity which they so materially contributed to bring about, was due not only to their remarkable capacity and industry, but to the confidence inspired by their scrupulous integrity and delicate sense of mercantile honor. It was this latter quality that gave them great power and influence in their widespread operations in different quarters of the globe, and enabled them to draw so many sources of wealth to the little seaport town which they had settled as their home and place of business. (85)

---

85. In Vol. IV, p. 456 of the *Magazine of American History*, is found a paragraph taken from the *Newport Mercury*, as follows: "In 1658, fifteen Hebrew families from Holland arrived at Newport, R. I., and brought with them the first three degrees of Masonry." The same statement, in identically the same language is contained in Dr. Fischel's "Chronological Notes on the History of the Jews in America," in the *Historical Magazine*, referred to in a former note.

But the most detailed account of the history of the Jews of Newport known to me is to be found in an interesting article by H. T. Tuckerman on "Graves at Newport" (*Harper's Monthly*, Vol. 39, p. 372). I glean the following from it: "On the 24th of August, 1694, a ship arrived at Newport, R. I., then the principal port of entry, from one of the West India Islands, with a number of Jewish families on board, of wealth and respectability, who settled there. In a few years a congregation of sixty worshiped in the synagogue, which at length boasted 1,175 worshipers. Gradually migrating to new States, not a resident Jew is now (1869) found in Newport—only their sepulchres remain."

"After the terrible earthquake at Lisbon, a company of Jews embarked thence for America; their precise destination was not settled, and the captain of the vessel on board of which they were passengers intended to land them on the Virginia coast. Adverse and violent winds led him to seek refuge in Narragansett Bay. Allured by the tolerant laws and spirit of Newport, the Israelite emigrants determined to remain there. Other Jewish emigrants from the West Indies and elsewhere followed their Portuguese brethren to Newport; and in 1763, when sixty families had settled there, the synagogue was erected."

It appears that in 1750 Moses Lopez was excused at his own request from all civil duties on account of his gratuitous services to the Government in translating Spanish documents. We also read that "in the early days of the Lopez establishment, his employees went out in boats and captured whales off the coast. Moses Lopez

Before the arrival of these enterprising merchants and their families, the religious exercises of the Jewish residents—their number being small—were conducted in private houses (86). But their number had now become large, and in 1762 the erection of a synagogue was begun, which was completed and dedicated in the following year, with great pomp and ceremony. Two years previously, in 1760, a learned young man from Jamaica, in the West Indies, came here, the Rev. Isaac Touro, who was chosen by the congregation as its rabbi, and under his teaching the synagogue continued to be crowded with worshipers until the breaking out of the American Revolution(87). It has already been stated that a burial ground was obtained in 1677. In that year a plot of land was conveyed for that pur-

---

at one time owned twenty-seven square-rigged vessels, and his correspondence indicates large and honorable commercial relations. Dr. Stiles loved to stroll along the Parade, discussing some point of Oriental wisdom with the learned Rabbi Isaac Carigal." As for the spermaceti oil and candle factory referred to in the text, our author states that "it was the first experiment of the kind in the colonies and was long a monopoly here, and no inconsiderable source of wealth. From Newport the enterprise was carried to New Bedford. "The war of the Revolution dispersed the Jewish merchants. Their ships were nearly all taken by the enemy."

Longfellow's beautiful poem, "The Jewish Cemetery at Newport," will be read with renewed interest in the light of these facts.—EDITOR.

86. Peterson, p. 181.

87. Rabbi Touro married a sister of Moses Hays, one of the Jewish merchants, and afterwards a very eminent merchant in Boston. The Rabbi was not only held in high regard by his own congregation, but was esteemed by his professional brethren of all denominations. With several he was upon terms of close intimacy, among whom may be named the celebrated Dr. Stiles, the President of Yale College, to whom he imparted a knowledge of the Hebrew tongue.

pose to Mordecai Campannal and Moses Packeckoe, which still exists, and as it is now enclosed, with its handsome wall and its Egyptian architectural gateway, is a conspicuous feature in Newport.

An event occurred in the year of the erection of the synagogue, 1762, which shows how readily prosperous communities may forget the liberal principles upon which they were founded, when the accumulation of wealth creates the desire to become aristrocatic and exclusive. Both Rhode Island and Maryland started with the broadest recognition of the rights of conscience as the prerogative and privilege of all who should settle there; and yet, in little more than a century, the one construed these rights as applying only to Christians, and the other as extending only to Christians of a particular denomination. When the Jews in 1684 applied to the Assembly in Rhode Island, they received the public assurance of that body, that they might expect as good protection in that colony as any other resident foreigners, (88) which was substantially declaring that no distinction would be made upon the ground of religion. In 1762, Aaron Lopez and Isaac Eleazar, being foreigners, applied for naturalization, which was granted, but afterwards set aside by a decree of the Superior Court as a direct violation of the Act of Parliament (13 of George II.,) they being Jews. The New England colonies at that time,

---

88. Arnold's History of Rhode Island, p. 478.

Editor's note: "Voted, in answer to the petition of Simon Medus David Brown and associates, being Jews, presented to this assembly, bearing date June the 24th, 1684, we declare, that they may expect as good protection here, as any stranger, being not of our nation, residing amongst us in this his Majesty's Colony ought to have, being obedient to his Majesty's laws." Proceedings of the General Assembly for the Colony of Rhode Island and Providence Plantations, June 24th,1682—Bartlett's Colonial Records of Rhode Island, III. p. 160.

1762, and during the fourteen years that intervened before the Declaration of Independence, did not trouble themselves much about the Acts of Parliament where they conflicted with their interests, or what they considered their rights, and even in this case the courts were not willing to put their decision upon the Act of Parliament alone, but proceeded to declare that, by the charter of Rhode Island, the free and quiet enjoyment of the Christian religion and the desire of propagating it were the principal views with which the colony was settled. This Arnold, the historian of Rhode Island, says was untrue (89), and the Court if they knew anything of the early history, knew it to be so. Probably conscious that this would not bear examination, they added another ground invoking the authority of the Act of Parliament, but construing it in a colonial sense, which was this: They declared that the Naturalization Act was designed for increasing the number of inhabitants, but as the colony was already full, it could not be the intention of the Act that any more should be naturalized, and consequently the naturalization of Messrs. Lopez and Eleazar was set aside. The two applicants had been residents of Rhode Island for many years before this, and admitting them to the privileges of freemen was not increasing the number of inhabitants, but the fact was that Rhode Island then, and for many years after it was an independent State, was a close corporation in which the proportion of freemen was not more than one in ten; a spirit of exclusiveness which was maintained in that State until it led in 1842, to what was known as Dorr's Rebellion, an act for which he was convicted of high treason, but which ultimately brought about the adoption of a more liberal constitution.

---

89. Arnold p. 496.

But the exclusion of the Jews from political privileges was not left to depend upon this judicial decision, and an act was passed in 1763 providing that no person who did not profess the Christian religion could be admitted free of the colony.

This was repudiating the act of 1652, that all men of whatever nation that were received as inhabitants of any of the towns, should have the same privileges as Englishmen, and the assurance given to the Jews particularly in 1684. Arnold says (90) that though the charter granted religious freedom, it did not confer political rights; but religious freedom can scarcely be said to exist when a man's religious belief is the ground upon which he is deprived of political rights. This illiberal course on the part of the governing classes in Rhode Island in no way affected the position of the Jews in Newport, or diminished the respect in which they were held in that town. They probably attached little value to the political privileges so jealously withheld, when they were not interfered with in the prosecution of their commercial pursuits, or disturbed in the practice of their religion, and, having the support and co-operation of their fellow-townsmen in their extensive mercantile operations, they not only increased in wealth themselves, but added to the wealth and prosperity of the community of which they were such valuable members.

The breaking out of the American Revolution put an end to the commercial prosperity of Newport. Its situation upon the ocean, which had made it before so favorable for commerce, had now an opposite effect, and left it more exposed to attacks from the enemy than any other place of equal importance in North America. Not only was its situation one of the most

---

90. 1 Arnold, 496.

exposed, but its inhabitants had especially provoked the hostility of the mother country, as it was one of the first places to manifest a spirit of resistance to the arbitrary acts of the British government by burning an armed vessel of war that came to exact an odious tax. In the then infuriated state of the British mind it could expect no mercy, and it received none. 8,000 British and Hessian troops occupied it, who destroyed 480 houses, burned the shipping, and during an occupation of three years cut down the groves and orchards, pillaged the library, then the finest in America, and carried off the town records. From this blow its commercial interests never recovered, and as the property and wealth of the Jewish residents was invested in, and formed part of the commercial capital of the place, the blow fell upon them with crushing effect. Aaron Lopez was a heavy sufferer, not only from what took place at Newport, but by the seizure of his vessels upon distant voyages, and by the deterioration of those that remained to him, by their being laid up for safety during the long continuance of the war.

The Jewish congregation being dispersed, the synagogue was closed, and Rabbi Touro went with his family to Jamaica, in the West Indies, where he died on the 8th of December, 1782, at the age of forty-six years. He left two sons, both of whom afterwards became very eminent merchants, Abraham D. Touro, who settled in Boston, where he died in 1822, leaving a very large estate ; and Jacob Touro, who went to Louisiana after its session to the United States, and became one of the wealthiest merchants of New Orleans.

When the struggle drew to a close, most of the Jewish residents had left Newport. Impoverished by the loss of their property, they sought other places in which to retrieve their shattered fortunes, and never returned. Aaron Lopez had retired with his family to Leicester, Mass., when the British army took possession of Newport, and remained there until 1782. The struggle was now practically over and he set out, intending to return and resume his business operations in Newport, but was destined never to see that town again. Whilst upon this journey with his family, on the 28th of May, 1782, he drove his carriage to the side of a pond to water his horses, resting upon what proved to be a quicksand, which giving way, horse, vehicle and inmate suddenly sunk to such a depth, as to render his rescue impossible. His body was afterwards recovered and brought to Newport, where it was interred in the Jewish cemetery, with every mark of public respect. Charles H. Russell Esq., to whom I am indebted for many particulars of the Jews of Newport, in detailing the accident by which this excellent man lost his life, writes: "Thus was removed in the meridian of life one of the most eminent and useful merchants that Newport ever had. His death, at the period it took place, may be considered as one of the greatest misfortunes that ever befel the town. Cut off as he was, preparing to renew his various enterprises, there can be no doubt from his extensive business relations, that had he lived, he would speedily have retrieved his losses and greatly contributed to revive the business and trade of the place. He was a man of eminent probity and benevolence. His bounties were widely diffused. They were not confined to creed or sect, and the people of Newport for more than half a century continued to venerate his memory." (91)

---

91. Considerable additional details about the Jews of Newport are to be found in "History of the Jews of Boston and New England" edited by A. G. Daniels. Boston, 1892. The author of the arti-

After the Revolution, a few families remained, and the services at the synagogue were continued until about the year 1790. The superior advantages of New York as the commercial centre and chief seaport of the country, became apparent upon the organization of the general government after the adoption of the Constitution of the United States, and as New York rose in commercial rank and importance, Newport steadily declined.

To the Jewish mind there is little or no attraction in a place, the trade of which is passing away, for the Jews have been for centuries a trading and commercial people. They are not without local attachment for the particular spot in which they have settled, and those who are past middle age may linger in the decline of its prosperity, but the young depart. As a people, they have dwelt almost exclusively in towns or larger cities for the reason that, except for a period comparatively recent, scarcely any other pursuits were opened to them, except those which were directly connected with trade or commerce. In most European countries in which they have dwelt, they have generally been denied the privilege of owning land, or, if permitted to hold it, it has been subject to such capricious and onerous exactions, as to prevent them from becoming agriculturists. They were equally shut out from mechanical pursuits. The mechanical arts were in Europe for centuries carried on under the supervision and control of guilds or corporations, who permitted none but those who were allowed to enter the organization to acquire a knowledge of or to practice them, and from their bodies Jews were almost uni-

cle has, however, failed to give the authority for his statements, and this fact, which is equally true of Markens'·"Hebrews in America," renders the work unsatisfactory and unreliable, for incorrect statements are joined with correct ones.—EDITOR.

formly excluded. Even after the system of guilds
was abandoned, Jews were not allowed even in so liberal
a country as Holland, to engage in mechanical
employments. By the municipal regulations of towns,
they were usually excluded alike from being mechanics,
or from keeping shops for the sale of goods by retail.
So stringent and uniform were these regulations,
that they were of necessity confined to migratory
trading, which among the poorer class would be peddling
or the loaning and exchange of money, and
the larger operations of commerce. To all this should
be added that in many of these countries, and for
centuries, they were subject at any time to be stripped
of their wealth, or, as not unfrequently happened, to
be suddenly expelled from the territory of the king,
or government, in a body with the power of taking
nothing with them but their movables. Under such
circumstances, there was little to attach them to the
particular country where they were born or dwelt, or
to create towards it, either in their own estimation or
in that of others, what is expressed by the word nationality.
There have been exceptional instances in
European history, such as the period of the Germanic
Empire, under Charlemagne; the dominion of Spain
by the Moors; Italy at intervals, and for a considerable
period Poland and Holland; but in most countries they
were subject to the disabilities above stated.

 This policy, which was designed for their conversion
or extirpation, produced an effect the very opposite
of what was intended. It made them more cohesive
and cosmopolitan, co-operating, acting and sympathizing
with each other, however widely separated
or extensively distributed, throughout the globe.

 Shutting them out from all other vocations and confining
them to trade and commerce, was to turn their
capacity and energies to pursuits for which, as an
acute, thrifty and intellectual people they proved to

be particularly adapted. From their cosmopolitan character they obtained a clearer insight and more enlarged views of what was requisite to promote trade in the intercourse between different countries, and to their comprehensiveness, quickness and sagacity is due in a large degree the discovery of the methods by which trade is facilitated and commercial transactions carried on at the present day.

The devotion of a whole race, widely distributed in different countries, to trade and commerce, especially when modern commerce was in its infancy, brought about results alike favorable to them and to the world. It gave them influence and power, and in the changes which commerce has effected—the intercourse it has promoted, the prejudice it has swept away and the advance in civilization that has followed it—they have played a more important part than has ever been adequately acknowledged.

The younger branches of the few families that remained in Newport, departed for other places, and settled chiefly in New York, Philadelphia, Charleston and Savannah. As no addition was made to the small Jewish population it was gradually diminished by death, until at last Moses Lopez, the nephew of Aaron, was the sole remaining Jew in Newport. Even he left and closed his days in New York, from whence his body was brought and interred in the Jewish cemetery, where the remains of his relations reposed.

He is said to have been a man of remarkable capacity, distinguished for his acquirements as a mathematician, his mechanical skill and his conversational powers. As a man of business he was noted for his uprightness, and is said to have been particularly earnest in his religious belief. His kinsman, Aaron Lopez, for many years the head and confidential clerk of the largest mercantile house in Newport, was affectionately regarded by his fellow townsmen of all denominations for his scrupulous integrity and interesting personal character. To these two excellent men should be added another of their representative survivors, a man familiarly known to all in Newport and greatly respected : Moses Seixas, the cashier of the Bank of Rhode Island.

The synagogue, after being closed for sixty years, was opened for public worship upon a single occasion in 1850, by a rabbi from New York. Abraham D. Touro, who, it will be remembered died in Boston in 1822, bequeathed by his will the sum of $10,000, as a fund for the perpetual reparation and maintaining of the synagogue, and $5,000 for keeping the street in front of it and of the burial ground, now known as Touro Street, in repair. The remaining son of the rabbi, Judah Touro, of New Orleans, in 1843, at an expense of $12,000, had the crumbling brick wall of the burial ground replaced by a substantial stone structure, the massive and imposing granite gateway of which, in the Egyptian style of architecture, is a conspicuous feature of Newport. It was but one of the many benefactions of this eminent philanthropist who, having amassed a fortune during a long life of sagacious enterprise as a merchant, bestowed the greater part of it upon public institutions and charities.

It has been mentioned that his uncle, Moses Hays, removed to Boston after the breaking out of the Revolution, and under his supervision Touro's life was passed at that place until his twenty-third year, when he went upon a voyage to the Mediterranean, as a supercargo of one of his uncle's ships. During the voyage the vessel was attacked by a French privateer, which resulted in a desperate conflict, and, what rarely happens in such encounters, Touro's ship came off victorious. In 1802, he went to New Orleans, where he passed the remainder of his life in a long and highly honorable mercantile career. He fought in defense of New Orleans, under General Jackson, in 1815, receiving a wound from a cannon ball, from the effects of which he never entirely recovered. Throughout his life, he was noted for his liberality and benevolence, contributing largely to charities, public institutions, and various enterprises, among which should be mentioned the donation of a very valuable lot of ground in New Orleans, for the erection of a Christian Church. He died there in 1854, at the advanced age of 79 years. Among other bequests he left $80,000 to found an almshouse in New Orleans ; $65,000 to the Hebrew congregations in that city; and smaller bequests to New York, Boston, Newport, New Haven, Hartford, Charleston and Savannah : $10,000 to the Society for the Relief of the Indigent Jews in Palestine; $50,000 for ameliorating the condition of the Jews in the Holy Land; $10,000 to the Jewish Hospital in New York; $10,000 to the Massachusets Female Hospital ; and smaller bequests to the Female Asylum and the Boy's Asylum in Boston. Nor was his native city forgotten. Among other benefactions to Newport he left $10,000 for the purchase of the antiquarian relic there known as the "Old Mill," supposed at one time to have been erected by the Norsemen, and the ground surrounding it, which, as now devoted to the public use, has been appropriately named "Touro Square." His body was removed from New Orleans to Newport, and rests in the cemetery there with the remains of his father and kindred. At the period of his death he had no known relations. His father came from Holland, and as the name would indicate, was probably a descendant of the Jews from Portugal, who sought and found a refuge in that tolerant land.

A large part of the fund left by these two brothers was designed not on'y for keeping the synagogue in continued repair, but a portion of it was specially intended for the annual support of a rabbi or minister. But there is no rabbi as there are no worshipers, and the interest upon the fund is year by year added to the principal. Newport from its salubrity, the beauty of its scenery, and the advantages it has for sea-bathing, became as its commerce declined, a place of resort for persons from all parts of the United States, during the heated months of the American summer, and is now, with its spacious hotels and streets of suburban villas, one of the most attractive and prominent watering places in America. It is sought alike by the pleasure-seekers, the votary of fashion, and those in pursuit of health; and among the mingled crowds that gather there in summer, there are doubtless Israelites. No one, however, known to be of the Hebrew persuasion, is found among the resident inhabitants; but the synagogue and cemetery remain, and through the fund erected for that purpose, will continue as permanent memorials of the Jews of Newport.

In 1819, a Mr. W. D. Robinson printed and circulated a pamphlet in London, entitled "Memoir, addressed to Persons of the Jewish Religion in Europe, on the subject of Emigration and Settlement in the United States of North America." The object of this publication was to induce the wealthier Jews in Europe to unite in a fund for the purchase of a large tract of land in the upper Mississippi and Missouri Territory to which the poorer classes of Jews throughout Europe might be sent to found an agricultural settlement. The plan was to offer to each Jewish emigrant a certain number of acres upon a credit for a specific number of years ; to convey the emigrants free of expense from Europe to New Orleans and then by the way of the Mississippi River to the place of settlement, to transport thither agricultural implements of every description. to be sold to the settlers on credit, and to establish rules and regulations for the general interest of the settlement and the reimbursement of the capital. The assurance is held out to the subscribers of the fund, that they will not only be rewarded by the grateful thanks of the settlers, but that as an investment it would ultimately prove of greater advantage and magnitude than any other mode by which funds could then be invested in Europe. The motive of the writer purports to be a benevolent one, and to have been induced by the oppressed and wretched condition then, of the great bulk of the Jews in Europe. I apprehend, however, that the writer, who styled himself in his title page "a citizen of the United States," was what is known in this country as a land speculator; for he takes occasion to inform his Jewish readers that there were then for *private* sale large tracts in the two sections he referred to, embracing several millions of acres adjacent to the Mississippi and Missouri Rivers. The Jews in Europe, who had accumulated wealth, were not of the class to instruct upon the subject of investing their capital. They were then, and have always been, far in advance of others in the knowledge of the means by which money can be turned to the best account. However desirous they might be to advance the interests and elevate the condition of their poor co-religionists, there was nothing in this scheme to commend it to them. It was in fact totally impracticable.

The Jews in Europe were not, and had not for centuries been, either artists or agriculturists, and to have transported a large number of these people, wholly unacquainted with the mechanical or agricultural arts, to a wilderness in America, to found a Jewish agricultural settlement, would have been a disastrous failure, like many analogous attempts in the early settlement of the United States. But the interested or enthusiastic Mr. Robinson, at the end of his pamphlet, held out the anticipation of a very different result from the adoption of his scheme. He presented the alluring picture, to use his own language, "of Jewish agriculture spreading through the American forests ; Jewish towns and villages adorning the banks of the Mississippi and the Missouri," and that "the arts, commerce and manufactures, would advance with the same rapidity in this new settlement, as had been exemplified in the agricultural regions of the United States." "Were I," he concludes, "to draw a picture of all the highly important consequences which suggest themselves to my mind, on this subject, I fear I might be called a speculative enthusiast." His fears were realized. The scheme evidently made no impression upon the shrewd, experienced and practical men, the wealthy Jews of Europe, to whom it was especially addressed ; for nothing came of it.

Certain portions of this pamphlet, however, are interesting, which relate to the condition of the Jews in Europe, sixty years ago, the extent of their emigration then to the United States, and the prospect this country held out to them. He pertinently remarks that among the immense variety and number of emigrants who had then come to the United States, either in the pursuit of gain or for political or religious reasons, very few had been of the Jewish persuasion, which he says, had arisen from a variety of causes. He remarks that the education and general habits of the Jews in Europe have fixed them in commercial cities and towns. That those who have acquired wealth live in luxurious magnificence and "consider Europe the only proper theatre on which they can exist and flourish." That those who have emigrated to the United States have been in general of the opulent class and pursue the avocation of their class in Europe ; that they were then (1819) the chief stock and money brokers in all the large cities of the United States and that it was rare to find one who was an artisan, and still more rare to see any who were agriculturists, or following rural occupations.

"The habitual propensity of the Jews," he says, "to engage in any other pursuits than agriculture, does not arise from the want of physical or moral energy, or any inherent aversion to cultivate the soil; but it is the effect of long continued social and political disabilities which has made it a matter of necessity with them for centuries, to limit themselves to avocations which can be pursued in cities and towns. If disposed to follow agriculture as a means of subsistence they are deterred by imperious difficulties, the chief of which in European countries has been the uncertainty that has attended their social and political state.

"If a Jew," he continues, "retires into the country, though surrounded by neighbors, he feels himself to be an isolated being, for he is cut off by existing prejudices from that social intercourse which is the chief felicity of man. Those who surround him deride or pity him. He has no synagogue that he can enter to adore his God according to the faith of his fathers, and therefore the constant disposition to live in cities or towns, where he can associate with his own creed and resort to a temple of worship, where he can fulfil what he conscientiously believes to be his religious obligations. How much worse," he adds, "is the condition of the poorer class surrounded by poverty and scorn, constituting no recognized link of the general bond that holds society together, and uncertain of reaping the precarious fruits of their personal industry. Hence is it, that the situation of that class in Europe is so abject and wretched We behold them carrying on the most menial occupations to gain a livelihood, and the means by which they gain it, besides being very precarious, do not suffice to furnish their families with more than a wretched pittance, and yet they are found under all these disabilities, to be an industrious, abstemious and persevering race of people. "To what part of the habitable globe," he says "can the Jews fly for an asylum, where will they be exempt from persecution and oppression? No part of Europe offers to them a secure or convenient refuge; nor can they seek it in Asia or Africa," and then remarks that the United States of North America, where the field for enterprise is immense, which is the only government among civilized nations that has wisely rejected any exclusive establishment, and where neither sect nor individual is molested on account of religion, is the only country upon earth that affords to them the means of regeneration, of security and comfort. (92)

Since these pages were written, thousands of Israelites who never read or heard of Mr Robinson's pamphlet, have quitted Europe and made the United States the home of themselves and of their posterity. In no country, except in France previously, had the same rights been conceded to them, in none had such a field been opened to them for individual exertion,

---

92. It would be interesting to learn how far, if at all this influenced Mordecai Noah in the formation of his scheme very soon afterwards of founding a Hebrew colony on Grand Island, in Niagara River. A detailed and very interesting account of this scheme will be found in Judge Daly's Supplementary Chapter.—EDITOR.

and in none have they in an equal period of time, augmented so rapidly. There are and have been for a long time, wealthier Israelites in Europe than in the United States, but in the United States material prosperity has been more widely diffused among them.

It is now nearly a century since the breaking out of the American Revolution, and during the whole of that time, Jews have enjoyed in nearly every State in the Union the same rights as all other citizens. For more than half a century the last vestige has disappeared in any State that made a distinction in its laws between them and others. This policy upon the part of the government of the United States and of the several States, has not only been beneficial to the Israelites and to the country that inaugurated it, but it has reacted upon Europe, and as a consequence of it, in most European countries nearly every restriction upon them has been swept away.

It has been remarked of the Jews that though hitherto retaining in all countries the characteristics of a distinct race, they have nevertheless imbibed and felt the nationality of the country where they were born or dwelt. Thus a French Jew is essentially a Frenchman, as a German Jew is essentially a German, or an English Jew, in appearance, feeling, and prejudice, is an Englishman. This is even more marked n this country, for none are more devoted to the Republican government of the United States than its Jewish citizens.

The Jews in the United States are estimated at about 300,000) in 1872), and something over one-third are assumed to be of native birth. As they enjoy here all the privileges of other citizens, as their children are educated in the public schools with the children of other denominations, and as in the cities they mingle constantly with all classes of their fellow citizens, in the relation of business and socially, it might be supposed that everything which marks them as a separate and distinct people would, under such circumstances. disappear. But this is a slow progress. Usages, customs and habits survive the causes that produced them, and that this assimilation does not take place as rapidly as might be inferred from these favorable influences, is due, not so much to any antagonism on the part of the people here or other denominations, as to the fact that the religious belief of the Jews is deeply incorporated with the family life; and thoughts, habits and feelings, that draw their vitality, as in the case of the Jews, from what has been recognized and adhered to in the family for centuries, are not easily given up. What is inculcated by the parents upon the child, as especially appertaining to the family to which he belongs, the child will very naturally when a man inculcate upon his offspring. A race so widely distributed over the globe, and so terribly persecuted in the past, owes its preservation and continuance as a connected body in a very large degree to what was cherished, maintained and inculcated in the family. The laws and the prejudices which have hitherto unjustly separated the Jews from the rest of society, have drawn them in closer communion with each other, and made the family with them both a social unit and a religious tie. Living essentially within themselves, they have never sought proselytes, nor sought to ally themselves with those who differ in race or creed. It is very remarkable that, whether living under free or despotic governments; whether suffering under restrictions which have isolated them as a separate or despised class, or born or dwelling in countries where there are no such restrictions and where they enjoy equally with others every individual and political right ; they still keep up their distinct characteristics; as a general rule, abstaining from connecting themselves by marriage with those who are not of their own denomination, as if instinctively avoiding to mingle their blood with other races. In France, since 1798, there has been nothing in the laws or in the course of the government, to distinguish them from other Frenchmen ; on the contrary, some of the most prominent men who have filled important positions in the French government, have been Jews. In the city of New York, for certainly one hundred years, the law has made no distinction on account of their religion, and in other cities of the United States, such as Philadelphia, Charleston, Savannah and Richmond, they have, at least since the American Revolution, enjoyed every privilege accorded to other citizens. But in all these cities, during this long period of time, as well as in France, there has been no marked change in this respect. The marriage of a Jew with a Christian is at the present day in the City of New York, almost as unusual and exceptional a circumstance as it was in the middle of the last century. Whether this will continue, or whether in countries where, as in France and the United States, the liberalizing effect of institution and the social and political equality, they are designed to bring about, will in time sweep away all distinctions, and produce a thorough co-mingling of the Israelites with other races, is one of those problems of the future, in respect to which no writer, in view of the historical past, is justified in expressing an opinion.

CONTINUATION IN 1893.

When I augmented my Address upon the Settlement of the Jews in North America, by the publication of a series of articles in the *Jewish Times*, it was my intention to close with an account of the settlement of the Jews in Richmond, Virginia, but I deferred the preparation of the final article, as the Rev. Jacques J. Lyons, who had been for a few years the minister of the synagogue Beth Sholom in Richmond, and was then in charge of the oldest Jewish congregation in this city, called upon me and manifesting great interest in my investigation,* proposed to procure for me all that was obtainable respecting the Jews in Richmond. I waited for that information for a considerable length of time, when I heard of his death, and would then have prepared the final article with such material as I possessed, but that the publication of the *Jewish Times* ceased very soon thereafter.

When the publisher of THE AMERICAN HEBREW expressed a desire to republish that which I had written, I promised to add to the publication what I would have done eighteen years ago, but for the causes above stated.

Upon looking recently, however, into Mr. Isaac Markens' work on "The Hebrews in America," published in New York, 1884, I find that this has been substantially done in the information there supplied (pp. 83-88). I could add something to it, but it would consist

---

*Mr. Lyons, who in conjunction with Rev. Abraham de Sola, published a work stated to be of great value upon the Hebrew Calendar, it has been said prepared for posthumous publication "An exhaustive history of the Jews in America, containing extremely interesting facts connected with their early settlement in this country," of which I know nothing beyond t' is statement.

only of dry details, which are not of interest to the general reader. All that I can do, therefore, to fulfil my promise to THE AMERICAN HEBREW to write a concluding part, is to add something respecting certain Jews of New York, who came within my own period, all of whom, with one exception, I knew personally.

The Jews of New York, from an early period in the present century were great patrons of the Drama; several of them were actors and three were successful dramatists. The first among the actors in the order of time, was Aaron J. Phillips. He was a native of Philadelphia, and made his first appearance in New York at the Park Theatre in 1815, and continued to be a member of the stock company of that theatre for some years. He was a comedian and a successful imitator of Barnes, a celebrated comic actor of that day. He and Barnes appeared as the Two Dromios, in Shakespeare's Comedy of Errors, and Phillips' imitation of the latter was so perfect, that it was almost impossible to distinguish one from the other. He was an uncle of Mordecai M. Noah, to be hereafter referred to; and Cowell, in his memoir, says, that through the influence of his nephew, who was then an editor and a successful dramatist, Phillips secured the part of walking gentleman, in which he says he was anything but interesting from his ungainly appearance, and that if a profile of his person had been taken in black, the difference could not be told between it and the shadow of a boy's top, with two pegs sticking out of it. His peculiar figure and face, however, were of service when he found his true role in grotesque comic characters. He was afterwards a manager of theatres in different cities in the United States, and was regarded as one of the best actors of old men upon the American stage in his time. He died in New York in 1826.

Another actor of the same name was Moses S. Phillips, who though, like the former, a native of Philadelphia, where he was born in 1798, was from his after associations, essentially a New Yorker. He made his debut at the Park Theatre in New York in 1827, as Mawworm in the "Hypocrite", and died in that city in 1854. He was also a manager of theatres in New York and other cities of the Union, in none of which was he financially successful from, it is said, his indolence and kind-heartedness.

EMANUEL JUDAH.

Emanuel Judah, who Brown, in his history of the American stage, says, was born in New York, was an actor of a higher type than either of the foregoing. He first appeared in New York for the benefit of Aaron J. Phillips in 1823, and was then announced as from the Southern Theatres, where he was always a favorite actor I saw him many times in Savannah in the winter of 1829 and have rarely seen an actor who was so uniformly excellent in whatever he undertook, and his range, within what is called the legitimate drama, was a wide one. He was a very gentlemanly man, below the medium height, with a finely proportioned person, a handsome face, and a voice of great sweetness, and power. Though he played attractively the higher parts in tragedy, he was most effective in melodrama and in what was then known as the romantic drama and was excellent in the leading parts in light comedy.

He was of that class of dramatic artists not very often found, who do everything well that they undertake without reaching the elevation of a great actor. He played occasionally in New York in different years, where, apparently, he was not appreciated as fully as he deserved to be, or as he was in the Southern Cities, where he was seen more frequently and in a greater range of characters. He was drowned in the Gulf of Mexico in 1839, upon a voyage from New Orleans to Galveston in Texas.

Mordecai M. Noah.

Among the dramatists, the earliest and most prominent was Mordecai M. Noah, who, as a journalist, an author, a politican, and as a public officer, was for many years one of the best-known men in New York. He was born in Philadelphia in 1786 and on the maternal side was of what in this country is looked upon as an old Jewish lineage, being a direct descendant of those Jews, who, in the early part of the last century, fled from Portugal to escape the torture, the dungeon or the faggot, and in one of his addresses he refers to an aged relative in this country, who, to the end of her life bore the mark upon her wrist, of the rack to which she had been bound. His immediate family, named Nunez, who were wealthy residents of Lisbon, escaped in an English frigate to London, from whence they emigrated to Georgia with Oglethorpe, and were among the founders of Savannah. The principal member of the family, Dr. Nunez, has been before referred to.

His relatives in Philadelphia had been active and influential supporters of the American Revolution and there was a tradition in the family that General Washington had been present at the marriage of his parents. Of his father, whose name was Manuel Noah, I know nothing, except that his son was left at the early age of four years to the care of a maternal grandfather; that when walking with this relative in the streets of Philadelphia he pointed out to him Dr. Franklin and his wife, and took him when a boy to the opening of Congress, where he saw Washington, of whom throughout his life he retained a vivid recollection. In Philadelphia he was put to the trade of a carver and gilder, which owing to his strong literary tendencies he did not follow, but found some other occupation, the proceeds of which supplied him with the means of going constantly to the theatres, in respect to which he made a statement worthy of the consideration of those who insist upon the immoral effect of theatrical representations. "I went," he says, "regularly to the theatre, rarely missing a night, and always retired to bed gratified and improved after witnessing a good play, and thus escaped the haunts of taverns and the pursuit of depraved pleasures, which too frequently allure and destroy young men. I have therefore, always been a firm friend of the drama"; in confirmation of which effect, I may add that, although Noah was constantly assailed for years during his career as a journalist and a politician, and sometimes by most vituperative epithets, I do not recall an attack assailing or in any way questioning the purity of his private life.

His fondness for the drama led him to join a juvenile company of amateurs, where his chief employment appears to have been the cutting up of plays, the substituting of new passages, the casting of parts and the writing of couplets for exits, and this youthful training in what is essential for dramatic effect, gave him a knowledge of what is requisite in the construction of plays, that dramatic authors do not always possess; which was thereafter his forte as a dramatist, and the reason why his plays were always successful.

In early manhood he went to Charleston in South Carolina, where he became, in 1810, the editor of a journal, *The City Gazette*, engaged actively in politics, and, it is said, studied law. Here the first of his plays was acted. He had previously written in Philadelphia a melodrama called "The Fortress of Sorrento," which, he says, was never performed. The one in Charleston he called Paul and Alexis," or, "The Orphans of the Rhine." It was written for Mrs. C. L. Young, an English actress, then playing in Charleston, who is described by Ireland as a perfect blonde with a profusion of rich golden hair, and of the rarest beauty of person. Though not remarkable as an actress, she was a great favorite, and this pretty play was doubtless written to heighten the attraction of her personal charms. It was afterwards taken to London by her husband, where it was altered and improved, and, with its name changed to "The Wandering Boys," was brought out in 1820 at the Park Theatre in New York with great success. It had the attracttion of two fine actresses, Mrs. Barnes and Miss Johnson. Mrs. Barnes, then and for many years one of the most distinguished actresses upon the American stage, as the fearless, intrepid and quick-witted boy, and Miss Johnson, afterwards Mrs. Hilson, in the character of his timorous and shrinking brother, says the aforementioned author of "Records of the New York stage," won universal applause, through the force and truthfulness of their acting, which I can affirm, having, when a boy, seen them both in this play, which for many years thereafter continued to be one of the most attractive and popular upon the stage.

Our naval war with Tripoli, which began in 1802, drew Noah's attention to the Barbary States. It led him to the study of the history of that part of North Africa from the Carthaginian period downward, and filled him with a strong desire to visit these States, as he said, "to seek out the ruins of Utica and trace, if possible, the field of Zama," the scene of Scipio's victory over Hannibal. There was another attraction: The Jews, from the time of the Romans, had settled extensively in North Africa, and their number had

been largely augmented by the persecution that drove
them out of Spain. To obtain authentic information
respecting this branch of the people of Israel, where
they were situated, their character, their resources and
their number, was to so earnest a member of that faith
as he was, a strong inducement; especially as no Jew
ish travelers, whose works were extant, had traversed
these countries since the journey of Benjamin of Tud-.
ela in the thirteenth century. But as these countries
were then inhabited by barbarians, it was not safe to
venture for such a purpose, beyond the limits of the
sea-board cities, without the security of an armed
force; and as this was always obtainable by a consul
such a position was desirable, and the Consulates of
Tunis and Tripoli were not then filled. He accordingly applied for an appointment to one of them, and as
he had been very active in politics in Charleston, and
had become quite prominent, he was able to bring so
much influence to bear in support of his application
that President Madison, while indisposed to grant his
particular request, offered him the Consulship of Riga.
This was an important commercial port on the Baltic,
but a continental war was then prevailing that would
have made the position an isolated one and he declined
the appointment. But two years afterwards, in 1813,
a state of things arose that enabled him to get the post
that he wanted. Though our naval war with Tripoli
was brought by our fleet to a successful end, and we
were in a position to dictate what terms we pleased,
our negotiations were so unskilfully managed by our
diplomatic representative, that we had to pay a considerable sum of money when the Treaty of Peace was
signed.

This greatly lessened the respect for us by the other
Barbary powers and especially on the part of the
Algerines. To secure our commerce in the Mediter-

ranean, we had for some years paid an armed tribute to this nest of pirates, but the large sum we had paid to Tripoli for a Treaty of Peace, after we had conquered it, led the Algerines to suppose that they could make more by preying upon our commerce, which had then become considerable in the Mediterranean, and they abruptly dismissed our Consul, captured a vessel from Salem and reduced the officers and crew, consisting of twelve persons, to slavery. This made it necessary to send out a judicious and competent representative to ascertain the real cause of this course on the part of the Dey of Algiers, as well as to secure the emancipation of our enslaved countrymen, and Noah was appointed for this important service. We were then at war with England, in consequence of which he sailed from Charleston in a vessel, bound for France, which was captured by the British fleet off the French coast.

The crew and some of the passengers were landed in France, but Noah was detained as a prisoner of war, and, being regarded as a person of importance was courteously treated by the officers of different vessels of the fleet to which he was successively transferred, until an opportunity was afforded of sending him to England; and when he arrived at Plymouth, this courteous treatment was continued and he was allowed to remain at liberty upon his parole. This enabled him to visit London and other English cities and to obtain considerable knowledge of the country and people. After some months he was released, and sailing for Cadiz in Spain, entered upon the duties of his office, which was that of Consul at Tunis, with certain powers in respect to Algiers. In Tunis he displayed considerable intrepidity and capacity in maintaining and securing successfully the right of asylum attaching to the Consulate, so essential in the general interest of humanity, in these arbitrary and badly administered governments.

After sufficient time had elapsed for investigation, he reached the conclusion and, so advised our government, that diplomacy could accomplish nothing with the Algerines. That a state of war would have to be recognized, and a sufficient naval force despatched to subdue them, which advice our government acted upon and sent out a squadron under Commodore Decatur.

By the written instructions of Monroe, who was then Secretary of State, Noah was authorized at some place, upon his way to Tunis, to devise means for the liberation of the American captives of Algiers ; to expend for their ransom any sum not exceeding $3,000 for each person, to find a suitable channel through which he could negotiate for their immediate release without its being understood to proceed from our government, but rather from the friends of the parties themselves, and, if successful, he was authorized to draw upon the United States Government for the ne cessary funds for the payment of the ransom of the captives and the expense of their return to the United States.

In pursuance of these instructions he found, upon reaching Cadiz, an American named Keene, who had been naturalized as a Spanish subject, and who was highly recommended to him by the American Consul there for this service. In employing him there was not only the advantage of his having the protection of a Spanish subject, but Keene was able, in addition, to procure despatches from the Spanish Government and special letters from the British Embassador at the Court of Spain, to the British Consul at Algiers.

Noah consequently engaged him and agreed to pay him, if successful, $3,000 for his services. Noah could not have gone himself in his diplomatic character to

Algiers, which would not only have been a departure from his instructions, but as the Algerines were then in open warfare with the United States, he would probably not have been recognized, and if he had gone there in any other character, and it was discovered that he was an American, he would have been seized and sold into slavery.

Keene, after an absence of six months, brought back with him six persons for whose rescue Noah expended $18,000, obtaining the money by drawing bills of Exchange on the United States Government, which he got discounted at Gibraltar.

But $4000 of the money was expended by Keene in Tunis. It was paid for the restoration of two of the twelve who had been captured with the vessel from Salem. The other four persons that Keene returned with had been brought to Tunis after Keene had arrived there. They were landed from a British frigate in Algiers and were consequently in the custody there of the British Consul. They claimed to be Americans and were probably natives of Louisiana. The British Consul was satisfied that they were Americans, and as an act of humanity, for, having openly avowed themselves to be Americans, they could have been seized by the Dey of Algiers, the Consul turned them over to Keene, who brought them away with him. Nothing was paid for them, and the balance, $14,000 of the money expended, was applied in the care of these six persons, which included sending them back to the United States and $6000 of it was paid to Keene, which was double the amount he was to receive by his contract. He told a long and complicated story, which Noah believed, of the difficulty he had to encounter, of the risk he ran of his life, and the expenses he had been put to, and Noah considered, in view of all the circumstances, that he was entitled to the $6000 that he claimed. The government, however, was not satisfied with the transaction, and, to Noah's consternation, the bills of exchange he had drawn upon it, came back protested.

Noah was placed in a critical position. He was responsible on the bills of the exchange as the drawer of them, and having no means to pay them, was liable to be arrested in Tunis and thrown into prison. No consul in Barbary would be recognized whose bills were known to have been protested by the government, and, as he states, he would have been left to starve for want of assistance and would have been subjected to insult and ill-treatment by the Berbers. He had no idea that the government conceived that he had gone beyond his instructions and supposed that the Department, when the bills were presented was without immediate funds to meet them; for during the war with Great Britain our finances were in a wretched condition and the credit of the government was greatly impaired, both at home and abroad. The protested paper, which with the loss and damage arising from the protest, amounted to over $21,000, was sent by the creditors to the British Consul at Tunis with positive and unyielding orders to seize the person and property of Noah for the payment of the bills. The Consul, however, was considerate and agreed to wait until the arrival of Decatur, believing with Noah, that he would bring with him the money to pay them.

Decatur's squadron arrived, and encountering an Algerine frigate, he captured it after a fierce battle in which an admiral who had long been celebrated in the Mediterranean and had become a terror to the Christian nations, was killed. Decatur followed this up by the capture of another cruiser, after which he blockaded Algeria so effectually as to cut it off from all access by sea.

This brought to terms the Dey of Algiers, who was compelled to sign a treaty dictated by the American Commander, by the terms of which all American captives were released and the United States relieved from any payment of tribute to those sea robbers thereafter.

This being accomplished, Decatur sailed for Tunis to enforce a claim for indemnity from the Bey of Tunis for surrendering to the English two of our prizes, which were lying in that port. Upon Decatur's arrival, Noah went on board his vessel and the commander taking him into his cabin, handed him a dispatch from Mr. Monroe, the Secretary of State. This Noah supposed would contain the explanation of the protests of the bills, but on the contrary, he found it to be a very curt letter, informing him that it was not known at the time of his appointment that his religion would be any obstacle to the exercise of his consular functions, but that recent information on which entire reliance could be placed, proved that it would have a very unfavorable effect; that the President, therefore, had deemed it expedient to revoke his commission, and that upon receipt of this letter he would consider himself as no longer in the service of the United States. To this the Secretary added that there were some circumstances connected with his accounts that required explanation, as those already given had not been approved by the President. This was a blow that would have unnerved any ordinary man; but Noah, in this emergency, showed the capacity and cleverness for managing a financial difficulty, that is characteristic of his race. A glance at Decatur's face satisfied him that the Commander knew nothing of the contents of the letter, and with that assurance he instantly devised a scheme to extricate himself from his pecuniary embarrassment. "If he had known," says Noah in the vindication, which he published, "what was contained in the letter, it would have been his duty, and which he would have exercised promptly, to have sent an officer on shore to take possession of the seals and the archives of the Consulate, and I would," he says, "have returned to Tunis stripped of power, an outcast, degraded, disgraced and with a heavy debt against me. I would, in all probability, have gone into a dungeon, where I might have perished, neglected and unpitied."

Quietly folding up the letter and putting it in his pocket, he proceeded to give Decatur a full account of the nature of our dispute with Tunis, explaining it with documents in his possession that he had brought with him. Having done this, he then suggested to the Commodore that, instead of going to the Dey himself and demanding the payment of the indemnity, he should leave the whole matter to him as Consul; that, as he had experience in dealing with these Berbers, he would be able more effectually to secure the payment of the money; and that, for that purpose, Decatur should give him a letter to the Tunisian minister, making a formal demand, as Commander of the squadron, for the indemnity. The great stake that Noah had at issue led him a little too far in the vehemence with which he urged this proposition, so as to attract the attention of Decatur, who could not understand Noah's anxiety that it should be left solely to him, as Consul, to obtain the money, when Decatur was there with his squadron, and could enforce the payment of it as effectually as he had brought the Dey of Algiers to terms. He suspected that some other motive dictated Noah's extraordinary warmth as he piled arguments upon arguments with such vehemence; and finally told him that if he imagined that he, Decatur, was there under his orders, he must undeceive himself. Noah quickly saw his peril. "It was evident," he says, "that a storm was gathering that would have destroyed all my plans," and with that adroitness he displayed throughout the whole of this transaction, he succeeded in calming our celebrated naval hero by the assurance that he wished mainly to co-operate with him in such measures as Decatur's own prudence would dictate, as they were both there to serve their country in the best manner they could. This satisfied the Commodore, who gave him the letter, and who upon the whole was pleased with the prompt way Noah pointed out of accomplishing the result the squadron had come there to bring about. It was then night; Noah betook himself to rest on the cabin floor, in a state of mind that did not invite repose, and, that there might be no opportunity for Decatur to reconsider his action upon more mature deliberation, the anxious ex-consul, at the earliest approach of dawn, got the officer of the deck to send him off in a boat to the shore.

On his way to Tunis he pondered over Monroe's letter, which he found difficult to understand, as the government was not only acquainted with his religion at the time of his appointment, but knew that it was one of the reasons why he desired it and it was not known in Tunis that he was a Jew. He states, what was probably true, that in the exercise of his consular functions he was not only respected, but even feared by the Tunisian government and enjoyed the esteem and good will of every resident.

He promptly submitted Decatur's demand to the Minister of Marine, who receiving it in no very good humor, sent for him and after declaring that this was not a proper and respectful manner of proceeding in such a matter, asked him why the American Commander did not come and make his complaint to the

Dey in person, and why he demanded an answer forthwith ; that they were not accustomed to be treated in such a manner ; that there was a time when the United States waited upon their pleasure to make a treaty, and not only paid for it, but gave them presents. Noah calmly answered that that was an affair of the past. That they ought to have complied with the demand of the United States before the arrival of the squadron ; that it was now too late and that Commodore Decatur had determined not to land without a favorable answer. "Why, Consul," said the Minister, "are you so tranquil? Before the fleet was here, you were loud and positive, but now that you are backed by a force, you suddenly become quiet and indifferent." "Because," said Noah, "remonstrance is no longer necessary. War is now inevitable. We have made peace with Algiers upon our own terms and the squadron is here for another contest, as it is better to have no treaty than one that is not respected." This was followed by an interview with the Dey, and the following morning the money demanded, $46,000 was sent to the Consulate.

Decatur naturally expected that the money would be given to him to carry back to the United States, and made inquiries as to his right to receive and retain it. But Noah was able to satisfy Decatur on this point, who supposed he was still the Consul. "I did not tell him," says Noah, "why I wished to retain possession of the money, or that I expected to be in America before he was." The purpose of the visit to Tunis having been accomplished, the squadron departed. As soon as it was gone, Noah paid the bills of exchange with the interest and damage, out of the money of the government in his possession, and leaving the Consulate in charge of a subordinate, he returned to the United States and settled in New York, where, in a few years, he became prominent as a journalist, and lived there for the remainder of his life. In going through Paris, on his journey home, it is said, that he accidentally met and recognized his father, whom he had not seen from the time that he was five years of age.

Immediately upon his return he went to Washington, and called upon Monroe, who, he says, received him ungraciously, and instead of a restoration as he expected, to an office of equal rank, accused him of going beyond his orders, of employing a most obnoxious character, of expending the public money unnecessarily, and justified his recall and the manner of it. This is difficult to understand as Noah represents it, for Monroe was an upright and a capable man and was not without experience as a diplomatic representative, having been our Minister to England, and as our Envoy to France had secured the acquisition of Louisiana. He was also a patriotic man who, when acting as Secretary of War, pledged his personal credit to obtain the funds that were necessary for the defence of New Orleans, and retired from the Presidency impaired alike in health and in fortune. John Quincy Adams said of him upon his retirement, that he was always honest and sincere; of intentions always pure, of labors outlasting the daily circuit of the sun and outwatching the vigils of the night; that with a mind always anxious in the pursuit of right he was patient of inquiry; patient of contradiction; courteous, always sound in his ultimate judgment and firm in his final conclusions, and it is difficult to suppose that such a man would treat Noah in the way that he did, unless there was something more than appears in the latter's narrative.

Noah, himself, acknowledged Monroe's high qualities, for in the vindication he published, he says that notwithstanding the treatment he had received at his hands, he advocated him for Presidency and sustained his administration, as he believed him to be an honest man and a patriot. But this was not as disinterested as it appears. Political consistency, or fidelity to party were at no time among Noah's characteristics. The fact was that there was no party at the time, in opposition to Monroe, to go to. The successful termination of the war, the effect of the holding of the Hartford Convention, and the rapid advance in the prosperity of the country, had completely overthown the federal party and it was then extinct. Monroe was elected President almost without opposition and was re-elected with more unanimity than any one since Washington, receiving every vote cast in the electoral college except one. In fact, the whole period of his administration is aptly described by the phrase then so often applied to it of "The Era of Good Feeling."

It took Noah a year to get his accounts adjusted, including several visits on his part to Washington, and when they were, he received a written acknowledgment from the adjusting officer that the government was indebted to him in a sum of over five thousand dollars. This was a recognition that he was justified in paying the amount of the protested bills out of the money of the government in his possession, and armed with this important document, he called upon Monroe who, however, refused to see him and turned him over to a subordinate.

When he settled in New York in 1816, Henry Wheaton, afterwards the distinguished author of the well known authoritative work on International Law, having been appointed a Judge of the Marine Court, retired from the editorship of the *National Advocate*, a daily journal that had been established by the

Tammany Hall party in 1813, and as Noah was out of employment and had had some experience in journalism in Charleston, he was appointed Wheaton's successor and continued to be the editor of that paper for nearly ten years.

In 1818, a new synagogue was erected upon the site of the old one in Mills Street, and Noah, upon its consecration, delivered the dedicatory address. In this address he referred to his family, stating that his grandfather, as pastor of the congregation, stood in the spot where he was then standing, seventy years before, and that his grandfather and his great-grandfather and his great-great-grandfather were buried in the cemetery before referred to in Chatham Square. The address was chiefly devoted to the past history of the people of Israel with an expression of the most positive conviction that the prophecy in respect to their restoration as a nation would be fulfiled. He pointed out how under every kind of persecution, they had still held together as a people, preserving their ancient faith; that there were then seven millions of them in the world, and that they would ultimately deliver the north of Africa from oppression, break the Turkish sceptre and in triumphant numbers would possess themselves of Syria. "This," he said, "is not fancy. I have been too much among them in Europe and in North Africa not to know their sentiments. They hold the purse-strings of the world and can wield the sword and bring an army of a hundred thousand men into the field."

This was with him no new idea. The restoration and re-establishment of the Jews as a people and the gathering of them together under the free and tolerant institution of the United States, was a subject upon which he addressed a letter in 1808 to Thomas Jefferson, to which the author of the Declaration of Independence made the pithy reply, that "intolerance is inherent in every sect; disclaimed by all when feeble and practiced by all when in power, and that our laws apply the only antidote, which is to put them all on an equality."

Noah's occupation as a journalist brought him into frequent connection with the theatre and led him to return to dramatic authorship. In 1819, he wrote for the Park Theatre, a clever play called, "She would be a Soldier, or the Plains of Chippewa," which from its own merit and the excellent acting of Barnes and Spiller in the comic characters, and that of Miss Leesugg, an English actress, in the part of the heroine, was a great success. Miss Leesugg, who shortly afterwards married James H. Hackett, the celebrated comedian and retired from the stage, is described as being at this time in the bloom of youth, with sparkling eyes, a buxom figure, a melodious voice, great sprightliness and vivacity, and as the very Hebe of actresses. As the heroine in this play, in which she appears to have been particularly attractive, she introduced, in the English translation, Hortense, the Queen of Holland's "Partant pour le Syrie," which became the French national air in the reign of her son, Napoleon III. In a rich contralto voice, she sang this romantic ballad with so much effect, that it became a favorite song in private circles for some time thereafter and underwent the unfailing test of popularity of being successfully parodied in a comic song, that was for years the delight of the circus. Noah in addition to this, wrote seven other plays, all of which, with one exception, were successful.*

---

* They were: "Marion or the Hero of Lake George," "The Grecian Captive," The Fortress of Sorrento," "The New Constitution," "The Canal," "Yesop Caramatti or the Siege of Tripoli." Hudson in his "Journalism," attributes to him four other plays, in some of which certainly and probably in all this writer was mis-

This was called the "Grecian Captive," which he wrote in 1822, for the benefit of his uncle, Aaron J. Phillips. Noah thought it would add to the attraction to present each person who went to the benefit with a printed copy of the play, which had a result he did not anticipate; for when the actors looked upon the audience and saw a thousand persons, each with a book in hand, turning over the leaves, with the accompanying buzz and flutter, they became confused, forgot their parts and to carry on the action of the piece, had to improvise, by saying whatever occurred to them, which had the effect, also, to confuse the audience in attempting to follow the dialogue, until a climax was reached by what the beneficiary thought would produce a great effect. This was the entry of Phillips, as the Turkish Commander, mounted upon a live elephant, that had been procured from a menagerie. His grotesque figure has already been mentioned, and as the huge animal, with Phillips perched on the top of it, came marching down to the footlights, to the alarm and confusion of the musicians in the orchestra, Phillips, unable to steady himself upon the unwieldly beast, toppled over and the curtain fell amid shouts of laughter from all parts of the house. Noah was greatly ridiculed for his production, and had the manliness to come out in his paper with a statement that the failure of his drama was not owing to the actors,

---

taken. They are Ali Pacha or the Signet Ring, which was written by John Howard Payne; the Siege of Dalmatia, by which was probably meant the Siege of Damascus, which was not written by Noah, but by John Hughes, in which Mr. Hosack, a member of a distinguished family, made his debut at the Park Theater in 1826, and neither he, nor the play, were ever heard of afterwards on the New York boards; "Natalie" which may refer to a ballet of this name that was first performed at the Park Theatre in 1839 and "Ambition" a tragedy, that was produced as a new play, at Burton's Theatre, in New York, in 1858, two years after Noah's death.

but to his own imprudence in furnishing each of the audience with a printed copy of the play.

In 1819 he published his "travels." He had been frequently assailed by political opponents for his acts as consul, and the object of this publication was not only to give an account of the countries he had visited, but to vindicate his official acts in Tunis. The work was well written, but badly arranged, as the narrative was given continuously without any division into chapters or any index, and his consular troubles and difficulties are mixed up throughout with his journeys and observations as a traveler. It contains a description of the different places he saw in England, France, Spain and the Barbary States, and much of the local history of the various cities and towns that he visited ; a kind of information that it was more difficult then to obtain than it is now. Sixty years afterwards, I went over the same ground that he traversed in Southern France, in Spain and a portion of North Africa, a part of the world that has since undergone comparatively little change, and can commend the acuteness of his observations, his general accuracy and graphic manner of describing what he saw. The work was well received, as it contained a very full and the best account that we then had of the Barbary States, which at the time in this country was of national interest, in consequence of our recent naval wars with Tripoli and Algiers.

He gives in it a very full account of the Jews in these States, of whom there were 700,000, about 60,000 being in the province of Tunis and from 20 to 30,000 in the City of Tunis. He describes them as the leading men in Barbary; that they were at the head of the Custom House, that they farmed the revenue, that they had secured the monopoly of various kinds of merchandise and of the exportation of different articles; controlled the mint and regulated the coinage, kept the Dey's jewels and were his secretaries, treasurers and interpreters; that they were the principal mechanics and that the little that was known there of arts, sciences and medicine, was confined to them; that many of them possessed immense wealth and many were poor; that the idea that they were oppressed, was in a great measure imaginary, and the general account that he gave of them, especially of those of Tunis, was not very complimentary. The fact which he states, that it was not known in Tunis that he was a Jew, although it was said that there were 30,000 of them in that City, would indicate that he deemed it advisable to conceal his religion, and that Monroe may have been right in his letter, that it would be on obstacle to the exercise of his Consular functions and produce an unfavorable effect.

He made a profitable use of the limited period that he was in Tunis in the study of antiquities and in archæological researches, which he embodied in his book. Among other things, he investigated the ruins of the Carthaginian city and what remained of a long past civilization in the immediate vicinity of Tunis, and thought he discovered the spot where the battle of Zama was fought, which resulted in the defeat of Hannibal by Scipio, and the overthrow of Carthage. Upon the whole, his book was a creditable one, and gave him a reputation both as a scholar and as an intelligent traveler.

In the ten years that elapsed after the publication of this book, he became prominent in New York both as an editor and as a popular dramatist; and George P. Morris, the editor of one of the earliest of our literary journals of New York, has given his recollections of him at this period. He says that he was then a great literary and political lion in the City of New York;

that he told the best story, rounded the best sentence, and wrote the best play of all his contemporaries'; that he was the life and spirit of all circles ; that his wit was everywhere repeated and that, as an editor, critic and author, he was looked up to as an oracle.

In 1820, he wrote a melodrama, called "Yusef Carmatti or, The Siege of Tripoli," which was produced at the Park Theatre, for the benefit of Miss Johnson, the attractive actress before referred to. This was his first and only attempt to obtain a pecuniary recompense for his dramatic productions, and on the third night of the representation of this play, May 25th, 1820, it was given for his benefit to a crowded and fashionable house. The performance was concluded satisfactorily, when, immediately after the audience left the house, it took fire, and in a very short time the theatre was burned to the ground. Fortunately, the receipts of the night were saved, having been taken by the treasurer to his own house before the fire broke out. On the following day the amount received, over two thousand dollars, was sent by the Manager to the author, and Noah, with a benevolence that was characteristic of the man throughout his life, gave the whole of it for the relief of the indigent members of the company, who, in consequence of the calamity, were for many months thrown out of employment. This act of generosity was highly commended at the time by citizens of every class, as it deserved to be, and especially as Noah was a man of but limited means, editors then being about as poorly paid as poets.

When the Park Theatre was rebuilt in 1821, Noah, as his contribution to the new edifice and to honor the annual celebration of the evacuation of the City of New York by the British in 1783, wrote a military play, which he called, "Marion or The Hero of

Lake George." He was then an officer of the New York militia, with the title, by which he was always known afterwards, of Major Noah, and to add to the eclat of the military drama and to the celebration of the anniversary, he exerted himself to procure a large attendance of his military associates in uniform, with a result that may be described in his own words: "what with generals, staff officers, rank and file, the Park Theatre was so crammed, that not a word of the play was heard, which was a very fortunate affair for the author."

In 1822 he was appointed Sheriff of New York, an office from which, during the short time he held it, he derived no pecuniary benefit, as he gave a large part of the proceeds to the widow of his predecessor in the office, who had been left destitute, and the residue and more, he expended for the relief of poor debtors, who as sheriff, he had in custody, imprisonment for debt then being allowed. By the amended Constitution of 1821, the office of sheriff was made elective, and Noah was nominated by the Tammany party for election. Meanwhile he had given great offence. He had applied for a portion of the state printing and failing to get it, made an unwarrantable attack upon some of the most respected leaders of the democratic party, charging them with the want of good faith, which caused such indignation that a formidable opposition was organized against him, and in one of the most exciting political contests, that New York had previously known, he was defeated. During the canvass one of the objections urged, was a Jew's being put in an office where he would have the right to hang a Christian; to which Noah replied in his pointed way, "that it was a pity that Christians had to be hanged."

As Monroe's administration drew to a close, the

political harmony that had prevailed, disappeared, and four candidates were brought forward for the presidency. John Quincy Adams, his Secretary of State, Wm. H. Crawford, his Secretary of the Treasury, Henry Clay, and General Andrew Jackson.

The Tammany party, or the Bucktails, as they were then called, supported Crawford and Noah in their organ, the *National Advocate*, denounced the Republicans who did not support Crawford, as traitors, which was meant to apply to the Clintonian party who sustained Jackson, and especially to Charles King, the editor of an influential republican evening paper called *The American*, who came out for John Quincy Adams, the personal antagonism of the two editors, King and Noah, being one of the political features of the time. General Jackson received a greater number of votes than either of his competitors, but lacking a plurality, the election devolved upon the House of Representatives and John Quincy Adams was elected President.

King's paper, *The American*, became consequently the organ in the City of New York of the new Administration, and the *National Advocate*, the leading journal in opposition. After the War with Great Britian, King, who had been sent out to England by the President, charged with certain duties respecting the American prisoners at Dartmouth, had done something to which Noah took exception, and with this cause of a quarrel, a controversy began between them which lasted for many years.

On the part of King, who was a high tempered man and vigorous writer, it was particularly vindictive, whilst on the part of Noah, who had a facile pen, it was clever, adroit, and most effective in the shape of short witty sallies and humorous retorts, and was carried on throughout in such a vein of outward pleasantry and inward sarcasm, as to be exceedingly annoying to his irate antagonist.

Many of his crisp and amusing paragraphs in this controversy might be given, but one will suffice to show their general cleverness. Madame Brugere, the wife of an opulent French merchant of this City, had become socially distinguished for her fine manners, queenly bearing and the elegant receptions she gave at her spacious mansion in Broadway. The lady gave a fancy ball, that is said to have been the first one ever given in America; which Scovill, in his account of the merchants of New York, says, set everybody crazy in the city, and that for months every one spoke in raptures of the great fancy ball. King, who was a man of social position, and whom Noah was in the habit of calling the pink of society, was invited and went to it. The ball was attended not only by the elite of New York society, but of Boston, Philadelphia, Albany and Baltimore. Noah in some way contrived to get an account of the principal persons who were present, and of the fancy dresses they wore, that he published in his paper, in which account he stated that King went to the ball in the dress of a private gentleman, and nobody knew him; that he changed his dress three times in the course of the evening, and being recognized in his last disguise, the band struck up "God Save the King."

The *National Advocate* was not what is called a paying paper, and as Noah's remuneration was small, and as he did not agree with one of the proprietors as to the manner in which the paper should be conducted, he left it in 1826 and established a daily journal of his own which he called by the same name, the *National Advocate*. This he was enjoined from doing by the court, when he changed it to *Noah's National Advocate* and this being also enjoined, he called it the *Enquirer*, which he continued to edit until it was merged in 1826 with the *Morning Courier*, under the joined name of the *Courier and Enquirer*.

It was the custom then both of the English and American newspapers to discuss the questions of the day in what are called leading articles. These he seldom wrote, as he was not clever in argument; but generally confined himself to short, pithy paragraphs, seasoned with humor and pointed by wit, which proved quite as effectual as graver essays.

He was quite a master of sarcasm, in the use of which however he was rarely malevoent or vindictive, but employed it as the most potent means for ridicule.

In 1825, Noah turned to his long cherished scheme of the restoration of the Jews to their past glory as a nation. Whilst a most tolerant and liberal-minded man in respect to the religious belief of others, he was strongly attached to his own people, regarding them as a race apart, originally chosen by God to work out a sublime faith, who, notwithstanding all they had undergone, were increasing in number and had a great future before them. He not only believed in the fulfilment of the prophecies, that they would come together again as a nation, but that the time in the world's history for the beginning of the movement had arrived, and that he, under Divine inspiration, was an appointed instrument to bring it about; for among all the successors of Israel and of Jacob that assembled in the synagogue, there was not one who was a more sincere believer or reverential worshiper.

For this purpose he acquired, with the aid of some of his friends, an island thirteen miles in length and about five miles broad, called Grand Island, in the Niagara River, which divides the northwestern part of the State of New York from Canada and is close to Niagara Falls. Here the down-trodden Israelites from all parts of the world were to be brought as an "Asylum" and "City of Refuge," who together with the North American Indians, whom he believed were the descendants of the Lost Tribes of Israel, were to form a great agricultural and industrial community, which was to be the beginning of the restoration of the Jewish people as a nation, under the constitution and liberal government of the United States.

That the American Indian, who is by nature a nomad, and the Jew, who since the dispersion of his people, even when free to do so, has rarely taken to the cultivation of land as a means of livelihood, could be welded together in a self supporting, agricultural community, was an idea that would never occur to any one of a practical mind; but upon this subject Noah was an enthusiast; and like many enthusiasts, did not trouble himself by looking at the practical side of the matter. In a memorial to the New York Legislature for the purchase of this land, he represented, that if the Jews in Europe were assured of such an "Asylum of Freedom" as he proposed to create upon Grand Island, they would emigrate to it in great numbers.

Subsequently he was not so confident of the co-operation of the North American Indians. Measures however, were to be adopted to make them sensible of their origin, to cultivate their minds, soften their nature and finally reunite them with their brethren, the chosen people.

This restoration of Israel as a nation, in and under the government of the United States, however, was not to be final. The Jew, he declared, would never relinquish the hope of gaining possession again of his ancient heritage in Syria, and that the founding of this Asylum in Grand Island, therefore, was merely "temporary and provisional."

It was, however, to be in this country, a gathering of the Jews together as a nation, from all parts of the world, and, as such, it required a directing power or head, which he considered could be accomplished by simply re-establishing the patriarchal form of government under which the children of Israel had lived in Palestine. If the Jews had ever in their patriarchal State any central head denoting national unity, it was not the high priest, but was in their fifteen successive judges, until the functions of the judges were vested by the people in a King, who was "to judge them" as well as to fight their battles. The term King however, was not an appropriate one to designate the head of an organization under a republican form of government, and Noah, going back to the judges, adopted the title of Governor and Judge of Israel. It was not exactly known how the judges in Israel were appointed, and Noah solved the difficulty by appointing himself to this high office, and as the self-appointed ruler, for this purpose, of the seven millions of Jews throughout the world, he fixed a day, the 15th September, 1825, for the dedication of the Asylum upon Grand Island, the laying of the corner-stone there with imposing ceremonies of the "City of Refuge," which he called Ararat, and he prepared to be issued, as of that date, his proclamation to the Jews throughout the world.

This extraordinary document, his proclamation, is too lengthy to be inserted here, but some account of it is essential to a full understanding of what he undertook and expected to accomplish, as well as of the character of the man.

It began stating to his "beloved brethren" throughout the world, that, whereas, in fulfilment of the promise made to the race of Jacob, they are to be gathered together from the four quarters of the world and to resume their part among the governments of the earth. Therefore, I, Mordecai M. Noah, citizen of the United States, late Consul to Tunis, High Sheriff of the City of New York and Counsellor-at-law, by the Grace of God Governor and Judge of Israel, have issued this proclamation. The document sets forth the great advantages of the State of New York, as a place of settlement for the oppressed and downtrodden Jews throughout the world, the fecundity of its soil and the salubrity of its climate, and especially of the attractions of Grand Island and of the beauty of its situation "where," he said, "they can till the land, reap the harvest, raise their flocks and enjoy their religion with peace and plenty" and these allurements having been pointed out, the document proceeds as follows :

"In His name, who brought us out of Egypt, I revive, renew and re-establish the government of the Jewish nation, and enjoin it upon all Rabbis, Elders of Synagogues, Chiefs of Colleges and all of the brethren in authority throughout the world, to circulate this, my proclamation, announcing to the Jews that an Asylum has been provided for them. It is my will that a census of the Jews be taken throughout the globe, and the returns registered in the Synagogues. Those who from infirmity or any other cause are willing to remain where they are,"he says, "are allowed to do so, but are to encourage the emigration of the young and enterprising, so as to add to the strength of the restored nation." He commands strict neutrality in the war between the Greeks and the Turks, which was then pending, and declares that those who are in military employments may remain. He abolishes polygamy, and directs that all prayers are to be read thereafter in Hebrew. The North American Indians, who, the document says, are admitted to be of Asiatic origin, and in all probability are the descendants of the lost tribes of Israel, are called upon to come and unite with their brethren, as the chosen people, and in the tolerant spirit of the man, those of other denominations are also allowed to come, if they desire to do so. He then imposes a tax of three shekels, or one dollar in silver, annually, upon every Jew throughout the world, to procure agricultural implements for, and to meet other expenses of the new settlement. He appoints by name a number of commissioners, in various cities in Europe, to assist in carrying out his proclamation, to whom proper instructions are to be transmitted thereafter, and finally, the brethren are asked to remember him in their prayers. After which the document closes with "By the Judge, A. B. Seixas, Secretary pro tem," which proclamation was, no doubt, as was its object, largely distributed throughout the world, where Jews in any considerable number were settled.

On the day fixed for the inauguration, the 15th day of September, 1825, it was found that there were not boats enough in Buffalo to carry to Grand Island all who wished to be present, and the celebration, in consequence, took place in Buffalo. The Jewish standard was displayed from a flag-staff. A procession, headed by a band of music, was formed, composed of military companies and several Masonic bodies in full regalia, after which came Noah as Governor and Judge of Israel in black, wearing a judicial robe of crimson silk, trimmed with ermine and with a richly embossed, golden medal suspended from his neck, followed by Masonic officers and dignitaries, who, with some citizens, closed the procession, which after marching through the principal streets of Buffalo, entered the Episcopal Church, the band playing the Grand March from Judas Maccabeus, and placed upon a table in front of the altar, was the corner-stone of the anticipated city, with this inscription, "Hear, O Israel, the Lord is our God. Ararat, the Hebrew Refuge, founded by Mordecai M. Noah in the month of Tishri, corresponding with September 1825, in the 50th year of American Independence." A prayer was delivered by an Episcopal clergyman, passages or lessons were read from the Old Testament, and Noah, in his robe as Judge and Governor of Israel, delivered an oration that filled more than five columns of the large sized journals of that day, which a contemporary Buffalo newspaper declared contained details of the deepest interest, to which the crowded auditory listened with profound attention. These details consisted of an account of the Jews in the various countries in which they had settled and an exposition of his scheme for their restoration as a nation, which I have already substantially given, and the exercises closed by the choir singing, "Before Jehovah's Awful Throne."

Afterwards a salvo of 24 guns was fired and a monument of brick and wood was erected upon the Island, on the site of the contemplated city, with the inscription, "Ararat, a City of Refuge for the Jews, founded by Mordecai M. Noah in the 50th year of American Independence.

The celebration in Buffalo was the beginning and the end of the scheme. The European Rabbis refused to sanction it. The proclamation was not responded to. The monument of brick and wood, like the project itself, fell to pieces, and in the course of years wholly disappeared.

General Jackson, in recognition of Noah's political

services, appointed him in 1829 Surveyor of the Port of New York. The Senate by a close vote rejected the nomination, but, upon Jackson's representation that some of the Senators who had voted against it had been misinformed as to certain facts, it was reconsidered, and after a severe contest, in which the Senate was equally divided, the nomination was confirmed by the casting vote of Vice President Van Buren.

He held this office until 1833, when he resigned it. His resignation was attributed by his political opponents to General Jackson's refusing to appoint him to the more lucrative office of Collector of the Port of New York. Whether this was true or not, he was from that time an active opponent of Jackson's administration. The *Courier and Enquirer*, under the joint proprietorship of Webb and Noah, had supported General Jackson for the presidency, and his administration during his first term. But Jackson, having followed up his veto of the charter of the United States in 1832, by his removal of the deposits of the bank in 1833, after his re-election, the *Courier and Enquirer* came out against him and became an organ of what was known for many years thereafter as the "Whig Party." This change was alleged by Jackson's supporters to have been brought about by a loan or gift to Col. Webb on the part of the bank of $50,000 to secure the influence of the paper in its favor. There was some grounds for the belief that the bank made unwarrantable use of its funds to secure political influence, and especially that of leading newspapers, and on an investigation by a committee of Congress, a promissory note made by Noah was found amongst the assets. Noah, in his testimony before the committee, stated that the money for which the note was given, was received from a private individual as a loan pressed upon him of unemployed funds, which was probably true; for no one, so far as I know, ever accused him of personal dishonesty; being a man, who in money matter, was always more ready to give than to take. In all probability, however, the note was brought to the bank by some one into whose possession it had passed, and the bank gave the money upon it to get Noah's influence, or to silence his opposition. He expressed to the committee his surprise, as he said, "to find his note turn up among the assets of the bank," and after this transaction, he withdrew from all further connection with the *Courier and Enquirer* and sold out his share of that paper to his co-proprietor, Col. Webb.

There was perhaps another explanation of Noah's coming out at the time against the administration. Jackson's removal of the deposits of the government from the United States Bank and depositing them in the state, or as they were called, "pet" banks, created a great sensation throughout the country, especially in all commercial circles, and particularly in the City of New York. There was the attraction, therefore, to a politician like Noah, of the formation of a powerful political party in opposition to the administration, which the "Whig" party rapidly became, to the building up of which he could largely contribute by the establishment of a journal of his own, and also accomplish another purpose. Van Buren was recognized not only by Jackson himself, but by the bulk of the democratic party, as the one who was to be supported as Jackson's successor in the presidency, and Noah, at this time, was at enmity with Van Buren, to defeat whose aspirations was to him then a desirable political object. Although he owed to Van Buren's vote his office of Surveyor, Mr. Van Buren afterwards prevented him from getting the office of State Printer, which was then, as it has been ever since, a political gift. Van Buren's influence secured it for Edwin Croswell, a member of a political junta, called the "Albany Regency," that had then the control of the democratic party of New York, and after this contest for the office of State Printer, an animosity arose between Noah and Van Buren that continued as long as both were living.

Upon leaving the *Courier and Enquirer*, Noah, in connection with Thomas Gill, who had been the business manager of the *Evening Post*, started a new paper, called the *Evening Star*, which was devoted to the "Whig" party. New York at that time scarcely admitted of three evening journals, but through the skilful business management of Noah's partner, Gill, the paper was successful. What Noah foresaw, the ultimate triumph of the "Whig" party, came about, but not in time to prevent Mr. Van Buren's succeeding to the presidency. After, it accomplished its purpose by the election of General Harrison as President in 1840. Noah's partner, Mr. Gill, died, and from the want of his efficient services, the circulation of the paper fell off; Noah sold it to one of his evening rivals, the *Commercial Advertiser*, and Governor Seward appointed him in 1841 an Associate Judge of the New York Court of Sessions. This was an office he was qualified to fill. He had to some extent studied law in Charleston and a general knowledge of the commercial law was not difficult to master. The office of a criminal judge, moreover, is one that requires in a greater degree than any other judicial station, the tempering of justice with mercy, and whilst Noah was an experienced man of the world, he was at the same time at heart one of the kindest and most benevolent of men.

He had no sooner, however, commenced the discharge of his judicial duties than Bennett, in the *New*

York Herald, began to assail and ridicule him. Scarcely a day passed, without some short article in which he was generally referred to, not by name, but by an abbreviated slang phrase, implying a dealer in second-hand clothing. His proceedings in court were misrepresented, his decisions caricatured and his religion frequently referred to, as if it were a matter of reproach. This course on the part of Bennett was the more remarkable, as it is said that Noah loaned Bennett the capital, $100, with which he started the *Herald* as a small sheet, Bennett being then employed on the *Courier and Enquirer*, and that it was 20 years before the loan was repaid. Noah himself made no complaint, but one of the jurors, attending the Court, was so indignant at this unjust aspersion of him from day to day, that upon his own motion he instituted criminal proceedings and Bennett was indicted for libel. When the case came on for trial in the Court of Oyer and Terminer, before Judge Nathan Kent, Noah appeared, and a scene occurred that was quite characteristic of the man. When the case was called, he rose, and addressing the court said that the attack upon him, by Bennett in the *Herald*, was the continuation of an old editorial quarrel, in which he had been to a considerable degree the aggressor and that so far as he was concerned, he was willing that the prosecution should be dropped. But the Judge would not consent. He directed the trial, to proceed and there being no defence, the jury found a verdict of guilty.

On the day fixed for the sentence I was in Court, and remember that the Judge, with much dignity and in an impressive manner, stated that the printing in a public journal, from day to day, of such grossly, abusive articles, in respect to a Judge who was engaged in the discharge of public duties, was not merely an offence against him, but one the tendency of which was to bring into disrepute the administration of the criminal law, and, which, in his opinion, should be punished by imprisonment, and that if it were in his power he would sentence Bennett to the penitentiary for the longest period the law allowed; but he had been, he said, overruled by his associates, the two aldermen sitting with him, and would pronounce, not his own, but their sentence, which was a pecuniary fine of a comparatively small amount.

Noah did not continue in this judicial office very long; after leaving it, he started a weekly journal in support of Tyler's Administration called the *Union*, that lasted about a year. He then became, and was for a considerable time, the editor of the *New York Sun*. During his connection with the *Sun* he edited a paper, subsequently known as the *Times and Weekly Messenger*; that he continued to be the editor of for the rest of his life, and under the title of *Noah's Times and Weekly Messenger*, it is still published, being now in its fifty-third year.

In 1840, he published a translation of the Book of Jasher, and before it wrote essays on Domestic Economy, which appeared in one of the newspapers he edited. In 1842, he was elected President of the Hebrew Benevolent Society, the institution in commemoration of whose 50th anniversary my address was delivered, and continued to be its President until his death. In 1846, he delivered an address which he afterwards published, to show that the American Indians were the descendants of the lost tribes of Israel. In this production he brought together a large amount of material, to prove the resemblance between them and the Jews in visage, customs, traditions and religious belief, much of which however, had been collected by earlier American writers, Adair, Boudinot, Ethan Smith and

Priest, in support of the same theory. Noah gave as his reason for this address, that previous writers upon the same subject, of whom, however, he names but one, Adair, though thoroughly informed respecting the rites, ceremonies, usages and belief of the North American Indians were not well acquainted with those of the Israelites, in which I think he undervalued the extent of the knowledge of some of his predecessors. The facts so brought together, he deemed convincing; but he was neither an ethnologist nor an anthropologist. Fifty years ago, even the first of these sciences, had made but little progress, and he did not know that distinction of races, or racial connection, is established by tests of a very different kind from those that he thought so conclusive. In 1845, he published what he called "Gleanings from a Gathered Harvest," which was made up of things he had written, and in the same year a monograph on the Restoration of the Jews.

Hammond, in his Political History of New York, has given his character. After remarking that much had been said and alleged against him, which he, Hammond, considered ill founded and undeserved, he added that his political, or rather, his party principles sat rather loosely, too loosely, upon him; but that he was frank, open, unreserved, generous and kind in his nature, and that his talents as a writer, especially as a wit, were of a high order. He died in the City of New York, on the 22nd of March, 1851, in the 66th year of his age, and while obituary notices of him, and some of them quite lengthy, appeared in the other daily journals, the *New York Herald*, though containing editorial obituaries of less important personages, did not even notice the fact of his death.

SAMUEL B. H. JUDAH.

Another Jewish dramatist and writer was Samuel B. H. Judah. He was born in New York in 1799, and was of an old colonial Jewish family that had settled in this city as early as 1725, and probably before it. His father, Benjamin S. Judah, after the close of the American Revolution, became one of the most prominent of the merchants of New York; a man greatly respected for his probity and valued for his enterprise and business abilities. He was one of the founders in 1786, of the New York Tontine, and in business corporations and in other institutions, held positions of trust and confidence. When the war broke out with Great Britain in 1812, he was a wealthy man, carrying on an extensive business with the West Indies, which was suddenly brought to end by the imposition of the embargo. As nearly everything he possessed was invested in a very profitable maritime commerce, the cessation by the embargo of all commercial intercourse by sea, came upon him so unexpectedly that he was unable to meet his engagements, was compelled to fail, and like many of the leading merchants of New York at that time, he was irretrievably ruined, for although he lived for many years thereafter, he never recovered from this overwhelming disaster.

In consequence, as I suppose, of the limited resources of his parents, young Judah had not the benefit of a collegiate education, but he acquired at one of the schools of the city, some knowledge of the classical languages, and was taught French by a well-known teacher of the time, named Boeuf.

As a young man, he had literary aspirations, which were directed towards the Theatre, and in 1820 he wrote a melodrama, entitled "The Mountain Torrent," which was produced that year, at the Park Theatre, with fair success. In 1822, he wrote another melodrama, "The Rose of Arragon," that was acted at the same theatre, and was much more successful. This was followed by another play, "The Tale of Lexington," and in 1823 a benefit was given to him at the Park Theatre, at which the two latter plays were acted. I know nothing further of his efforts as a dramatist, and presume that he had not become sufficiently successful as a playwright to induce the managers of the Park Theatre to bring out any more of his productions, as in a publication of that year, he complains of Manager Simpson's want of education, as an explanation of his inability to appreciate his, Judah's merits.

The publication referred to, which appeared in 1823, was entitled "Gotham and the Gothamites, a Medley." It was a versified production assailing over a hundred persons, who were then more or less prominent in the City of New York, assuming to be written in the interest of virtue and morality, but which from the motive that led him to write it, and the means he employed to bring it into notice, is almost without a parallel in the history of defamatory literature. The satirical productions of Churchill and of Dr. Wolcott, better known as Peter Pindar, were then read more than they are now. They were popular, and it was doubtless from an ambition to achieve the kind of distinction these writers had attained, that led him to conceive that a production in verse, grossly calumniating every one in New York who was at all prominent, would bring him into great notoriety.

But Churchill and Wolcott had, what he had not, the literary merit that is shown in the telling couplets and biting satire of the former, and the exquisite humor and felicitous versification of the latter; in addition to which, the first of these clever satirists in verse had the redeeming quality, that he could praise as heartily as he could censure.

To their eminence, vain as he was, Judah could scarcely hope to attain; but there was another model that pointed out to him a way by which he could do in prose, what he had not the ability to accomplish in verse. A few years previously, in 1819, Gulian C. Verplanck, published a political satire, commonly known as "The Bucktail Bards," under the *nom de plume* of Major Pindar Puff. This was a satire in easy flowing verse, directed against prominent persons in the political party, then known as the Clintonians, and their distinguished leader, DeWitt Clinton, who were satirized by ludicrously exalting them and by ridiculing under the form of affected praise the pretensions of Clinton to scientific knowledge and great literary attainment. Unlike Judah's productions however, there was nothing malevolent or vindictive about it, nor anything in the form of scurrility, or personal abuse. As a distinguishing feature, it had at the end of each epistle, copious notes, and as Mr Verplanck was a man of learning and of some humor, these notes added much to the effect of the verse; and it was this method of Mr. Verplanck's in the form of notes, that Judah followed, as a more effectual means, by which he could abuse and slander the persons he attacked.

The poem was devoid of literary merit. He had very little knowledge of metre and lacked an ear for distinguishing rhyme. It was consequently marked by halting verses and imperfect couplets. There was a mawkish sentimentality in many passages that he conceived to be poetry, in which moonshine and the adjuncts of the theatre, were substituted for nature, and there was an effected assumption of morality and virtue, that was as false as it was meretricious.

I have said, that nearly everyone that was then prominent in New York, was referred to and slandered;

public officials, politicians, merchants of the highest integrity, eminent lawyers, editors, clergymen, booksellers and publishers, literary men, professors in colleges, actors, theatrical managers, prominent military men, scholars and artists. No one was omitted, the attack upon whom he supposed would create a sensation. They were not referred to by name, but the first letters of the Christian and surname were given, and the omitted letters in each were indicated by asterisks or stars, so that it was easy for any one then familiar with the prominent people in New York to know who was meant, and, after a lapse of seventy years, I have been able, out of the one hundred and three persons referred to, to identify ninety-eight.

As the great bulk of the personages mentioned were people of character and blameless lives, there could be no motive for dragging them before the public, and calumniating them, except the one that has been suggested. As to some of the others, he appears to have had an antipathy, or a feeling of personal enmity, which was especially the case toward his coreligionist, Noah, and what he published respecting him will suffice to show the vituperative character of the production. He is generally referred to as "this fellow," "A writer of Linsy Woolsy Paragraphs and Still-Born Lumps of Stupidity." * * * "A pertinacious scribbler of insipid garbage." * * * "A smirking, wriggling, smiling thing who says his plays were not all hissed, which was because his audiences were unable to hiss and could only gape. * * * Who damns the worth he cannot equal and never blushes except when, unawares, he stumbles upon a truth."

Immediately upon the publication of the book he caused handbills to be posted up throughout the city, offering a reward for the discovery of the author, and wrote anonymous letters to a considerable number of persons he had mentioned in it, which, save in the adaptation of each letter to the particular person addressed, informed them generally that the work had appeared; of the large sale of copies of it on the second day of its publication, which was untrue, and earnestly advising them to take immediate measures through the newspapers, or otherwise, to vindicate their characters from the unjust aspersions cast upon them. One of these letters was sent to Col. W. L. Stone, the editor of the *Commercial Advertiser*, who, upon reading it, was struck with its resemblance to a communication that a short time before had been sent to him for insertion in his paper. It was a literary review of the seven leading authors of America, and as Judah's name was the third or fourth on the list, the experienced editor came to the conclusion that a review placing Judah in so eminent a position and prophesying that from the talent he had already displayed, how much might be expected from him in the future, could have been written by nobody but Judah himself, and Colonel Stone laid it aside not intending to publish it. Upon comparing this article with the letter he had received, he found that both were in the same handwriting, and purchasing a copy of the book, he, with this proof, went before the Grand Jury and had the author and publisher indicted for libel. The arrest of both a few days after the publication put a stop to any further circulation of the book, and the publicity of the criminal proceedings brought to light a number of the like kind of letters which Judah had written, all being in the same handwriting, which were given up to the public authorities.

The publisher made no defence, but Judah employed counsel and under the pretense of absent witnesses that he required to prove a justification, or a matter in mitigation, he got the trial put off for several terms, until at last, Hugh Maxwell, the district attorney, who was an energetic officer, brought the cause peremptorily to trial, when, there being no defence, a verdict of guilty was rendered, and a substantial fine was imposed, which Judah being unable to pay, he was sent to prison.

He had some pulmonary affection which, being augmented by his imprisonment and the great heat of the weather,—it was in the month of August, —brought on a severe attack of illness, and as the physician of the prison certified that he would not probably recover unless he was released, the Governor granted him a pardon and he was discharged. A few years afterwards he became a lawyer. How the author of such a production as "Gotham and the Gothamites" succeeded in getting any respectable lawyer to certify that he was a man of good moral character, which was indispensable to an admission to the Bar, I do not know, but he certainly obtained such a certificate, as he was admitted an attorney and counsellor of the Supreme Court, and was for many years a practitioner.

He was not unfrequently before me in my earlier years upon the bench, and exhibited no ability as an advocate. He had the habit not uncommon at that period with some New Yorkers, of substituting the 'w' for "v," such as "If the gentleman will wouch for it on his weracity, etc," and this peculiar pronunciation together with the unattractiveness of his personal appearance, and his lack of ability for constructing a speech, made an unfavorable impression upon jurors, of which, from his earnestness, he appeared to be wholly unconscious.

As an attorney, a gentleman who had much to do with him in the transaction of business, described him to me as acute, cunning, technical, and not very reliable; notwithstanding which he was able to obtain what, in those days when imprisonment for debt was allowed, was called a collecting business, by which he was able to secure an ample competency, on which he lived for the rest of his life.

He published a work of fiction which was not of any particular merit, the scenes of which were laid in the earlier part of the Colonial history of New York, the name of which I cannot now recall. In his last years he was a great sufferer from some chronic disease, and died in the City of New York about the time, I think, or shortly before the breaking out of the civil war.

JONAS B. PHILLIPS.

This continuation has extended so far beyond what I expected, that I will close it with an account of another Jewish dramatist of New York. This was Jonas B. Phillips, who first appears in connection with the drama in 1833, as the author of a spirited epilogue written for the benefit of A. A. Adams, a tragedian of great merit, who appeared that night in John Howard Payne's tragedy of "Oswald of Athens," at the close of which Mrs. Hughes delivered Phillip's epilogue, with great effect.

In 1838, he produced a melodrama called "Cold Stricken," and though it had the attraction of Mrs. Barnes and Judah, the versatile actor before referred to, it was not very successful, but was appreciated by the managers, who gave the author a benefit.

He afterwards wrote a play called "Camillus," and a drama, "The Evil Eye," which was produced at the Bowery Theatre in New York with great effect, and had what is called a run.

He had, I think, some position in connection with the business management of this theatre, and produced other dramas there. These were of a spectacular kind, in which as a playwright he was very successful. He was much esteemed among the theatrical people with whom he was associated, and in 1835 a complimentary benefit was given to him in that theatre, when several prominent actors and actresses and distinguished musical artists appeared and made it a success. After this, he withdrew from all connection with the theatre, studied law, and in the course of years became Assistant District Attorney for the City of New York.

It came within my judicial duties to preside frequently in the Court of Sessions in the absence of the Recorder, so that I saw much of Phillips, who was an honest, a most industrious and an efficient public officer, for whom I felt a personal regard. He filled this office during the term of several district attorneys, and died in the City of New York about fifteen years ago.

Having mentioned the Court of Sessions, I may appropriately refer to another officer of that Court, of the Jewish persuasion, Jacob Hays, the High Constable, who as the head of the constabulary force of the City of New York for nearly half a century, had an influence and control over the criminal classes, like that exercised by Townsend, the celebrated Bow Street officer, for so many years in London. Hays was a short, stout, thick-set man of unswerving honesty, untiring energy and indomitable courage. Scovill refers to him as the most remarkable man that New York ever produced, and certainly within his own sphere of activity that city has never had one like him, before or since. The criminal classes both feared and respected him, which they well might, for he was the very embodiment of that fine characteristic—a high sense of duty, and the name which they gave him of "Old Hays" was for years a "terror to evil-doers."

The act re-organizing the police force of New York, dispensed with the office of High Constable, with this reservation, however, that in view of his long and faithful services, he was allowed to retain both the title and emoluments of the office for the rest of his life. The only duty under the act that was left to him, was to sit in his wonted place in the Court of Sessions, below the Judge, during the sitting of the Court, which he discharged with unfailing regularity up to an advanced age; an interesting and picturesque figure, with his bright, penetrating eye scanning every one in the audience and turning it upon each person as he entered. When the loud call of the crier announced that the sitting was over, and that every one might depart, the venerable High Constable turning towards me would say, with an old-fashioned dignity of manner, "Have I kept order, sir, in the Court?" and receiving the usual affirmative answer, he would retire with the firm step and steady carriage of a veteran athlete, and with his retiring figure before my mind, I am admonished that the period has arrived to close my account of the Settlement of the Jews in North America.

APPENDICES.

APPENDIX I.

DOCUMENTS RELATING TO THE ARRIVAL AND SETTLEMENT
OF THE JEWS IN DELAWARE.

From the Minutes of the Adm'n of Jean Paul Jacquet, Vice-Director at the Delaware, and his Council, 28th Dec., 1655:

Treaty made for trade with the Indians on behalf of the community living at Fort Casimir, which they willingly assented to, and each subscribed to a subsidy with the exception of Isaac Israel and Isaac Cardoso, who refused to give their consent and prepared to leave the river and give up their trade, than to assist with other good inhabitants in maintaining the peace of this highway. Document Relating to the Colonial History of the State of New York, XII p. 136. Among the subscribers is *Master Jacob.*

On June 16, 1656, " Isaak Israel appears against Jan Flamman and presents the following petition:

To the Honbl. Vice-Director and his Council residing in Fort Casimir

Showeth with due reverence the petitioner, Isaak Israel, that he, the petitioner, made an agreement with Captain Jan Flamman to bring him, the petitioner and his goods, to the South River; that he, petitioner, promised to pay to him, Jan Flamman, one anker of brandy, and satisfied him also before the departure: that, as he shipped two pieces of duffel more than was agreed; he, the petitioner, had promised, to give one beaver more and above the foregoing; but that, as by great improvidence and in fair weather the bark stranded during the night and remained there for a considerable time, whereby they were compelled to unship all the goods from the said bark and to bring them ashore, during the time they remained there, there was drunk and eaten by the ship's crew, as well as by passengers, of his, the petitioner's, goods—one anker of brandy and 15 pieces of cheese; likewise was his duffel much spoiled as in consequence of the stranding, tents and shipping places had been made of it. These damages can hardly be borne by me, even though the same had occurred through bad weather or other misfortune. It is estimated by me as follows:

for one anker of brandy—8 beavers,	fl 64
15 cheeses at 5 fl the piece,	75
for damage to the duffel, as the same has been discolored by rain and sunshine and otherwise,	200
Total amount,	fl 339

If any one should be of opinion that this damage was calculated too high, the petitioner promises 100 guilders and more to him, who shall replace his goods at his valuation, which they had at the time of shipping at the Manhattans, and while he would and must be well satisfied with the great loss of ship and goods if the mishap had occurred by unavoidable necessity, yet as he is still asked for the beaver, which he promised for the two pieces of duffel, besides all damage and loss which he has sustained, this quite unreasonable matter has induced him, the petitioner, to push his claim, therefore, he, the petitioner, turns to your honor, and requests that by your Honor he may be assisted and helped to his just and lawful claim, which doing, etc.," was signed, Isaque Israel.

The defendant answers that he has no knowledge of the points in dispute; was lying in his bunk, and acc'g to the statement of Captain Martyn, there was still 18 fathoms of water when he went to lie down in his cabin. As regards the brandy this was broached with the good and free will of the pl'ff, as the crew were wet and cold; he said, "Drink as much as is necessary, if that is empty you can get more; the stuff is lost anyway." As to the cheese, the plaintiff has dealt them out voluntarily to every one.

Whereas from these verbal discussions no certainty can be had, it is ordered that the parties adduce proof of their assertions.

On the 23d of June, Isaak Israel against Jan Flamman. The pl'ff produces the following affidavit: To-day, date as below, appeared before me A. Hudde, Secy appointed by the Hon'ble Lord and high Council, upon request of Isaak Israel, the Worshipful Lucas Dirco and Abraham Rycke. They declared together and each for himself and made affidavit, as they do hereby, that it is true, that they, being on board the bark, called "de Fenix," between the 14th and 15th of April, towards daybreak, weather and wind being fair, ran ashore and remained fast, and that during the time they sat there, one anker of brandy of the aforesaid Isack Israel was drank out and some cheeses eaten, but the number is not well known to them, as all the drinkables and eateables were taken for the satisfaction of their wants, without regard as to whom they belonged. Likewise, we know, that there were tents to lay under, and hammocks to lay in, made of his, Isack Israel's, duffels. They gave as reason of their knowledge that the affiants had been on board the bark during the time, which, as above written, we the undersigned declare to be true and truthful, and are willing to confirm, if necessary, with our oaths, and have signed this in presence of the below-named witnesses. Done at Fort Cassimir this 16th of June, 1656, in the S. R. N. N. It was signed Abraham Riycke, Luyck Dirco. On the margin stood, as witnesses, Jan Juriaensen, Jan Eckhoff. Having heard the arguments of the parties and their reasons pro and contra having been well stated, we cannot but judge that the matter necessarily must lead to a considerable increase of lawsuits, which again will give rise to others. The parties are advised, therefore, to arrange the matter in friendship, but if they cannot agree, they shall address us again. This they accepted. Doc. Relating to Colonial History of New York, XII. p. 147-8. Doc. R. to the H. of Dutch and Swedish Settlements on the Delaware. By B. Firnow.

Letter Wm. Beeckman to Stuyvesant. (XII, p. 447.)
ALTENA, the 5th of Dec. 1663.

GENTLEMEN.—I heard at New Amstel yesterday that Mr. d'Henojossa would send as quickly as possible a savage to your Hon'ble Worships, his Honor arrived here in the ship "de Purmerlaender Kirck," on the evening of the 3d inst., together with

Peter Alrichs and Israel, who went away with Miss Printz, as members of the high Council and 150 souls."

(Alexander d'Henojossa was appointed Director of the D. W. I. Co. colony on the South River. XII., p. 456.)

"The fur trade has been recommended to Mr. Peter Alrichs, who has brought along for it 200 pieces of duffels, blankets and other goods nec'y for it. Alrichs is to trade at New Amstil, the Honble Councillor Israel at or near Passajongh, etc." Dec. 28, 1663.

Census of Responsible Housekeepers and their family at various places on the Delaware River in 1680. (XII., p. 646-8.)

In St. Jones and Duck Creek :
    Mr. Isaack, 3 in family.
    Richard Levy, 2 " " (P. 647.)

APPENDIX II.

NOTES ON THE HISTORY OF THE JEWS IN ENGLAND AND THE AMERICAN COLONIES.

On September 12th, 1883, Dr. Felsenthal, of Chicago, sent a letter to Judge Chas. P. Daly, of New York, expressing his thanks for, and his appreciation of the admirable address which the honorable Judge had delivered a few months previous, at the laying of the corner-stone of the new Hebrew Orphan Asylum, in New York, and which address had afterwards been published in pamphlet form. After the assurance of his gratification and thanks, Dr. Felsenthal continued :

"Only in order to show you with what attention I have read your address, I beg to say that it seems to me you were not quite correct when you stated (on page 8) that 'Jews were not entitled to vote for members of Parliament.' This, it appears to me, conveys an error. By an Act of Parliament, passed 1740—13 Geo. II c. 7—which Act lies at this moment before me,—Jews living seven years in any of the American colonies were declared to be fully emancipated, and all rights of natives were granted to them, and they were deemed, adjudged, and taken to be his Majesty's natural born subjects of this Kingdom, to all intents, constructions, and purposes, as if they, and ever one of them, had been, or were born within this Kingdom.' Section 3 of this Act provided that in the oath of allegiance to be taken, Jews may omit from this oath the words 'upon the true faith of a Christian.' You see that this Act, so strangely overlooked by all historians of Judaism, though it is probably the very first legislative enactment in all Christendom in favor of Jewish 'emancipation,' in favor of granting perfect equality before the laws to the confessors of the Jewish faith—left nothing to be desired by the Jews in the American colonies in regard to their juridical and political status.

It would now be of interest to learn whether practically the law was carried out, or whether it remained a dead letter; whether it proved to be a stimulant to bring at that time a considerable Jewish immigration to these shores, or not, etc. An examination of the Court Reports of the Colonies, in as far as still accessible, might also contribute some knowledge on these points.

The historian of American Judaism will also have to deal with the curious fact that, while the Jews in the Colonies were admitted to full citizenship already in 1740, yet in some of 'the States' they were excluded from the enjoyment of the rights of citizenship by constitutional provisos. Thus, f. i., according to the old Constitution of Maryland only 'Christians,' or 'Trinitarians'—I do not remember which the word was—were eligible to State offices, until some fifty years ago a new Constitution was adopted. In North Carolina, until a few years ago, only Protestants could be elected to State offices. If I am not mistaken, all the States have now finally based ther constitution and laws on this point upon a true Jeffersonian basis, and have totally done away with the mediæval idea of placing the Jews upon the level of pariahs. But a query permit me: Is it not still held as a judicial maxim by some of the American jurists that 'Christianity is a part of the common law of our country?'

I hope, dear sir, you will excuse this letter. Please consider it as a tribute of thanks and of respect which I bring to you. With the highest regards etc., etc.

B. FELSENTHAL.

JUDGE DALY'S REPLY.

84 Clinton Place,
New York, November 30th, 1883.

DEAR SIR.—I owe you an apology for not answering your letters before. They were addressed to me during my Summer vacation, when I was absent, and since my return to this city, I have not had leisure until now to reply to them.

I infer from your letter, that you have not read the account I gave of the settlement of the Jews in North America, in an address I delivered eleven years ago (1872), on the fiftieth anniversay of the Hebrew Benevolent Society, and which, as subsequently written out by me, and augmented, was published in 1872, in successive numbers of the *Jewish Times* of this city. If you had, you would have seen that I referred to Tomlin's Law Dictionary, Art. "Jews," 4th London edition as authority for the statement that in 1737 (erroneously printed in my last address as 1728). Jews were not entitled to vote for members of Parliament. As Tomlin's Law Dictionary is a book for which you might have to seek in a lawyer's library, I will give you the passage in which he states the disabilities that Jews were under in England, as late as 1835, when the fourth edition of his work was published. It is as follows: "A Jew is prevented from sitting in Parliament holding any office, civil or military, under the Crown, or any situation in corporate bodies. He may be excluded from practising at the bar, or as an attorney, proctor, or notary, from voting at elections. from enjoying any exhibition in either university, or from holding some offices of inferior importance."

The Act of Parliament of 1740, to which you refer (13 Geo. II c. 7, Evans Stat. Vol. I., p. 10), had not much effect. Under it, foreigners who had resided seven years in a British colony, without being absent at any time over two months, might be naturalized; and if such foreigner were a Jew, he might be naturalized without taking the Sacrament of the Lord's Supper, under 7 Jac. I. c. 11, and in his case, under this Act, the words in the abjuration oath, "on the true faith of a Christian" might be dispensed with ; but the naturalization could only be obtained by applying for an Ac- of Parliament, and a certificate had to be obtained from the Home Secretary before a bill could be introduced that the person applying was of good character, etc. And as the procuring of the passage of an Act of Parliament was "attended with a great deal of trouble and some expense," very few Jews availed themselves of it, a fact ascertained by an enquiry made by Parliament in 1754 (Smollett's "History of England," B. III. c. III

5, X.). As this Act of 1740 applied only to persons who had resided the prescribed number of years in British Colonies, an act was introduced in 1753 (26 Geo. II C. 2) by which any foreign Jew could be naturalized upon like conditions. It passed the House of Lords without opposition, but was furiously assailed in the House of Commons. It was carried, however by the power of the Ministry. This Act, which is historically known as "The Jew Bill," continued only for a few months, for it was received by the nation, the historians tell us, with "horror and execration." Those who had voted for it were denounced by the people. The Bishop of Norwich was insulted at the communion, and in the public streets; petitions poured in from the cities for its repeal, and on the first day of the next session, a bill to repeal it was introduced and hurriedly passed with the assent of both parties. This intolerance in respect to the Jews continued until 1825, when an Act was passed (9, Geo. I. V. c. 27) relieving persons to be naturalized thereafter from the obligation of taking the Sacrament of the Lord's Supper.

So far from the legislation to which you refer having brought about any tolerant feeling towards the Jews, the repeal of this Act of 1753 was rather approved of than otherwise by Blackstone (1 Blackst. Com. 375), and in 1786, Lord Chancellor Thurlow decided that the bequest of one Isaacs, who left £1,200 to found an annuity for the support of a synagogue, was void, that the Crown should decide to what charitable use the annuity could be applied; and the Crown directed that £1,000 of it should be paid to the treasurer of a foundling hospital, to be applied towards the support of a preacher and the instruction of the children under the care of the hospital, in the *Christian religion* (Da Costa v. De Pays, Ambler's Rep. 228, Note 1, and see 7 Vesey, p. 61), which was the Government's interpretation of the testator's intention.

The account I have given you of the Act of 1740, of the hasty repeal of the law that was enacted afterwards to enable Jews to be naturalized under it, and of the intolerant spirit of the English people towards the Jews up to the end of the firs quarter of the present century, will, I think, be a sufficient reply to your inquiry respecting the effect of the Act of 1740. In 1737, a question arose in the colony of New York, whether Jews could vote for Members of the House of Assembly, it appearing in an exciting election that several Jews had voted for one of the candidates. The question was brought before the House of Assembly, and counsel was heard upon it on both sides, after which a resolution that they could not vote for Members of the Legislature was unanimously passed by the House, which had all the force of a statute. It was in these words: "Resolved, That it not appearing to this House, that persons of the *Jewish religion* have a right to be admitted to vote for Parliament men in Great Britain, it is the unanimous opinion of this House, that they ought not to be admitted to vote for representatives in this colony."

Before the passage of the Reform Bill and the repeal of the Corporation and Test Acts, which removed so many of the Jewish disabilities, it was never definitely settled what were the exact civil rights of Jews born in England.

In 1684, it was agreed before the King's Bench by the Attorney General, in the case of the East India Company v. Sands (2 Shower's Rep. 371), that all Jews in England were under an implied license, which the King might revoke, the effect of doing which would be that they would then become aliens. Even so great a Judge as Lord Hardwicke, held in 1744 that a bequest for the maintenance of an assembly or synagogue for the reading of the Jewish Law was void, because the Jewish religion was not tolerated in England, but only connived at by the legislation (3 Swanston's Rep., p. 489, Notes).

It was conceded that a Jew born in England, especially of parents who were also born in England, was a British subject; but whether he could lawfully hold real estate, was doubted. In 1818, Sir Samuel Romilly said that Jews born in England were as much entitled to hold land as any other natives, and that no one had ever objected to a title on the ground that the owner was a Jew, and many eminent lawyers and judges had before expressed themselves to the same effect; and yet, down to he removal of all disabilities in 1853, this point was still doubted under the statutes or ordinances of the 54th and 55th Henry III. (A. D. 1269), which declared that no Jew should hold a freehold, and was never definitively settled. Being a British subject and entitled to hold land would not, in itself, enable a Jew to vote for Members of Parliament at the period named (1737). Persons then entitled to vote for Members of Parliament were burgesses of the town or city represented by the member; or in the counties, persons who had a freehold estate yielding forty shillings annually; or those who enjoyed the right under some special franchise. Now, if a Jew were admitted to be a burgess of the town or city, or if he had a freehold estate yielding forty shillings annually, he would still, before voting for Member of Parliament, have to take the abjuration oath, if it was required (Watson on Sheriffs, p. 329). This oath was " on the true faith of a Christian," except in a few particular cases where these words, by statute, might be omitted, and this oath no Jew could take. This continued to be the law until the Act of the 8th and 9th of Victoria C. 52, by which these words, "on the true faith of a Christian," might be dispensed with, where the person swore that he professed the Jewish religion, and had conscientious scruples against taking the oath in the previous form. What Tomlins therefore meant when he says in the extract that I have given you, that a Jew could not vote at elections. was, that he could not, because he could not take the abjuration oath, which might be required of him.

The Jews in England were the very last to raise any questions, during the seventeenth and eighteenth centuries, about their civil rights. All they wanted was to be left undisturbed in their business, their families, and in their religious worship. They knew how hostile the English people were to them' especially after 1755, and being secure in their business, and undisturbed in their religion and their families they were exceedingly careful to avoid everything that might direct public attention to them as a body, or in any way excite the general anti-Jewish prejudice. So mindful and careful were they to divert any outburst of popular feeling from themselves, that during the Lord George Gordon riots, in 1780, the Jews in

Houndsditch and Duke's Place wrote upon their shutters: "This *house* is a true Protestant."

I trust, my dear sir, that you will find in the above statements all the information you desire in your letter.

I am, dear sir, very truly yours,

CHAS. P. DALY.

B. FELSENTHAL.

APPENDIX III.

On Some 18th Century Strictures on the Jews of New York.

There is an unfavorable statement respecting the Jews of New York, in the middle of the last century, in a small work published in London in 1765, called a "Concise Account of North America, etc., etc., by Major Robert Rogers."* It is contained in his description of the City of New York, and is as follows: " This city abounds with many wealthy merchants, who carry on a large trade to foreign parts and are observed to deal very much upon honor, excepting some Jews who have been tolerated to settle there, having a synagogue in the city, who sustain no very good character, being many of them selfish and knavish and (where they have an opportunity) are an oppressive and cruel people."

As this statement, so far as I have been able to ascertain, is unsupported by any other evidence, I have been at some trouble to gather what now can be collected respecting Major Rogers, the author of this book, as the weight to be attached to so serious a charge against a class of merchants of a particular religious denomination would depend upon the writer's means of information, and as we do not know what means he had, we would naturally be influenced in considering what reliance could be placed upon his statement by what is known respecting his character.

He was born about 1730, in Dumbarton, New Hampshire. His father was an Irishman, being one of the early settlers of that place. In early life he became distinguished in Indian warfare, and was the commander of a Corps called "Rogers'

---

*A concise Account of North America, containing a Description of the several British colonies on that continent; including the Island of Newfoundland, Cape Breton, etc., as to their situation, extent, climate, soil, produce, etc.; to which is subjoined an account of the several nations and tribes of Indians, by Major Robert Rogers London, 1765. 8vo.

Rangers," among whom were some of the hardiest sons of New England, General Stark of Bennington, Samuel Putnam and Ebenezer Webster, father of the celebrated Daniel Webster. In command of this corps, he served in the French and Indian war, and as a military leader was a man of courage and capacity, being successful upon two occasions in 1758, over great odds.

After the French and Indian War he went to England, and during his residence there underwent considerable privations. He managed, however, to borrow money to enable him to print his journal and the book above referred to, which he dedicated to the King. The work was commended by the *London Monthly Review*, the reviewer, in all probability, getting what knowledge he had of North America from what he found in the book. The dedication to the King proved of service, and Rogers was appointed Governor of Michillinacinock. He was there accused of plotting to plunder the fort and to join the French, and was sent to Montreal in chains, where he was tried by court-martial. What was the result of the trial I do not know, but he was in England again in 1769, when he was imprisoned for debt, and afterwards, according to his own account, was in the service of the Dey of Algiers, and fought in two battles. When the American revolution broke out he was in America, where, although making loud professions of patriotism, he was by the order of Washington arrested and imprisoned as a spy, and afterwards released by Congress upon his parole. When set at liberty he broke his parole, and joining the royal troops organized a corps called the "Royal Rangers," of which he was the Colonel, a corps that was celebrated during the contest. In 1778 he was proscribed and banished by an Act of New Hampshire, after which he went to England, and of his subsequent career I know nothing, except that it is said that he died there about 1800.

To break a parole is regarded by mankind as the most dishonorable act that an individual can commit. All recognize that this relief to the horrors of war would not continue to exist unless from its universal observance. The most depraved recognize this, and even savages. A military man, therefore, especially, who would break his parole, is one thereafter not to be trusted or believed in anything. I should attach no weight to the statement of the dishonored soldier respecting the Jewish merchants of New York at the period referred to, unless it was supported by some other evidence, and as I have already said, I know of none. On the contrary, the little that I have been able to find respecting the Jews of the City of New York at that time is favorable. Judge Thomas Jones*, the Tory historian of the American Revolution, in describing what he calls " the golden age of New York," which was this very period, says: "Even the very Jews all lived in perfect peace and harmony, enjoying the company and conversation of each other, and upon all occasions returning mutual acts of friendship, kindness and affection."

It may have been that this impecunious man, for such Jones appears to have been from all we know respecting him, borrowed money from one or more of these Jewish merchants, and was subjected to imprisonment, as was then allowed, to compel the repayment of it.†

CHAS. P. DALY.

---

*Jones' History of New York during the Revolutionary war, Vol. 1, p. 2.

†There is some evidence, but it is of a slight and indefinite kind, that there were some Jews who may have been in New York during this period, who were referred to unfavorably. It is contained in an advertisement in a New York journal of the date of September 5th, 1756, of Solomon Hayes, a Jewish West India merchant of the city, stating that "several scandalous Jews" were trying to hurt his "character and credit" as they had "done already," in which he offers a reward of 100 pistoles, a large one at that time, being over $300, to any person who would give intelligence as to "who they were and where they were;" and as he did not know them or where they were, they may not have been residents of New York.

INDEX.

Abrahams, Joseph, 72.
Adair, 137, 138.
Adams, A. A., 145, John 63, John Quincy, 63, 116, 125.
Adler, Prof. Cyrus 54; note 58.
Agriculture, Jewish, 92, 94.
Albany, 20, 22, 126; note 19; see Orange (Fort)
Algiers, 107, 121.
Ambrosius, Moses—held in default of payment, 7, 23; note 3,
Amsterdam, centre of religious toleration, 3.
Andros, Governor, 26.
Antwerp, treaty of, 3.
Ararat, city of refuge, founded by M. M. Noah, 129, 132.
Arnold, historian, 83, 84.
Astor, John Jacob, employed by Hayman Levy, 53, 54.

Bahia (St. Salvador) captured 5—resources and religious toleration, 5.—Jews settle there 5–6
Baltimore, 64, 126.
Bancroft, George xiv, 13, 62; note 67
Barbary States, 106, 107, 111, 121.
Barnes, Mrs., 102, 106, 119, 145.
Barsimson, Jacob, protests against taxation,, 17, 18, 19, 23; note 16,
Beekman, William, 34, 153.
Bellamont, Lord, antagonized 28; assisted by Jews, 28.
Benjamin, Abraham, 78; note 84—Isaac 78, note 84
Benjamin of Tudela, 107.
Bennett, James Gordon, 135,
Blackstone, 158,
Boeuf, 139.
Bonan, Simon, freeman, 27, note 25.
Booth, historian, 39.
Bornal, Raphael, 68, note 75.
Boston, 81, 86, 90, 91, 126; notes 87, 91.
Boudinot, 137.

Brackenridge, 62; note 66.
Brazil—settlements in, xiii,—Dutch occupation of xiii, xv, xvi, xvii, 5,6.
Breda, treaty of, 49; note 54.
Brodhead, Mr., cited, 1.
Brown, (?) 103, David, 82; note 88, Saul, complains about trade restrictions, 24; minister of congregation, 28.
Brugere, Madame, 126.
Bryson, David, 44.
Bueno, Joseph, permitted to trade in N. Y., 27 note 25.
Buffalo, 131, 132.
Burgher Guard, Jews in 16, 17.
Burial grounds, 34—permission for extension of land, 35—description of first cemetery, 35; notes 41, 43, 46—in Newport, 81, 82, 86, 91.
Butcher, Joseph Isaacs, 49; note 54

Cadillac, La Motthe, on sects, 26.
Cadiz, 108, 109
Campannel, Mordecai, 82.
Cardoso, Benjamin 22; note 18—Isaac, 22; note 18, 151.
Cardoza, Abraham Nunez, 76, note 82.
Carigal, Isaac, Rabbi, 81; note 85.
Casimir, Fort, 151.
Census of Jews in Barbary States, 121, in Florida, 75, note 82; in Georgia, note 82; New England, note 82, in Newport, 79, New York, 52, 58, 75; note 82; North Carolina, 75; note 82; Pennsylvania, note 82; South Carolina, note 82; in U. S. 97.
Characterization of Jews, 87, 97.
Charity of an early Jewish settler, 2, 23.
Charlemagne, 88.
Charleston, Jews settle in, 70, 71, 75, 76, 89, 91, 99, 105, 107, 108, 118; note 82.

INDEX

Charter of liberties and privileges, 25.
Churchill, 140.
Clay, Henry, 125.
Clinton, De Witt, 141—Governor, 51—Lady, 51.
Coen, Jacob, 20.
Cohen, Aaron, 78; note 84.— Abigail, David, Grace, Hannah, 68; note 75—Isaac, 68, 78; notes 75 and 84—J. Meyers, 31; note 32—Moses, 76; note 82—Nathan, Solomon, 78; note 84—Solomon, M., 60
Columbus, xi, xiii.
Commerce, its influence upon religion, xiv.
Constitution of U. S., 87.
Costa, D., 31; note 32, Jacob, 68 note 75.
Cowell, 102.
Cowyn, Jacob, taxed, 19; note 16.
Crawford, Wm. H., 125.
Croswell, 135.
Curacoa colonized by Jews, 9, 14.
Curtis, George William, 77; note 83.

Da Costa, Anthony, 65—Daniel Nunez, 45—Isaac, 76; note 82—Joseph, 19, 23; note 16—vs. De Pays, 158.
Daly, Judge, his address before the Hebrew Orphan Asylum, v, first publication of his work, v, its merits, v, xi.
Daniels A. G., 86 note 91.
David, Joshua, Sr and Jr., 49, note 54.
Davis, Richard, 40, 41.
Dandrade, (D'Andrada?) Fusilador, 19, note 16.
D'Andrada (Dandrada?) Salvator, denied the right of buying real estate, 18,19; note 16, 20—applies for citizens' rights, 23, 48, note 54.
De Beauchamp, xvii.
Decatur, Commodore, 109, 111, 112, 113, 114, 115.
De Fonseca, Joseph Nunez, founds a colony in Curacoa, 9.
Dekay, Jacob, 39, 40.

De Illan, Jan, 9.
De La Motta, Dr. Emanuel, 72, note 79.
De Lancey Oliver, 51.
De La Simon, Abraham, fined for violating Sunday laws, 11, 23, note 10.
Delaware, 22, 151, 154.
Delaware River, see South River.
De Lucena, Abraham p. 10 15—applies for charter, petitions for trade,18, 19, 20, 23, 24—trades to Lisbon, 28, 29.
De Lyon (Delyon?), Abraham, 66, 68, 70, 73, note 75.
De Meyer, William, 41, 42.
De Olivera, David, 76, note 82.
Depass, Abraham, 72 — David Lopass, 68, note 75.
Depivea, Aaron, 68, note 75.
De Sille, Nicasius, on Jews trading on the Delaware River, 20, note 17.
De So'a, Abraham, 101.
Disagreements between English and Dutch, 16.
Discovery of America, xii.
D'Medena, Isaac, 31, note 32.
Dongan, Governor, petitioned by Jews for more religious freedom, 25—not granted, 26, 27, note 25.
Dutch occupation of Brazil, xiii, xvii.
Dutch West India Company, xv, 5, 6, 9

Editor's work explained, ix.
Eleazar,Eleazer,78; note 84—Isaac, 78, 82, 83, note 84.
Elias, David, naturalized, 45; note 49.
England, excludes Jews from legislature, 47, 64, note 54.
English Jews, 97, 108, 157 -161.
Esopus, 22.
Expulsion of Jews from France, Spain and Portugal, 2.

Felsenthal, Dr. B., 155.
Fischell, Rev. Dr. A., xiv, 31, 80, notes 32 and 85.
Flamman, Jan , 151-153.

INDEX.   167

Fletcher, Governor, 27-Florida, 75.
Fonseca, Joseph Nunez de, 9.
Franc (Franci?) Jacob, 78, note 84.
France, 96, 97, 99, 108.
Franklin, Dr., 104.
Franks, Abraham, 31; note 32— Jacob, 31, 34, 43; note 32.
Frera, David, petitions for trade, 19, 23, note 16.

George I. issues an edict of naturalization. 49; note 54
George II. act of, 82, 154, 157.'
George IV. act of, 158.
Georgia—Jews in, 64—prejudice against Jews, 65—Moravians and Scotchmen in, 67, 75; note 82
Germany, 88, 97.
Gibraltar, 110.
Gideon, Benjamin, 68, note 75.
Gill, Thomas, 135.
Gilman, S., 75, note 82.
Gomez, Abraham, 54—Daniel, 30, 41, 42, 43, 44—David, 30, 41, 42—Isaac, Jr. 44, 54, note 58—Louis, traffics to Lisbon, 29, 34, 42—Mordecai, 30, 31; note 32, 41, 42, 43; note 43— Moses, Jr. 31; note 32.
Gomperts, Joseph, 70.
Gordon riots, 160,
Gould, N. H, Esq., 78, note 84.
Grand Island, 90, 128, 130, 131, note 92,
Gratz, Joseph, 61—Michael, 60, Rebecca—the supposed character in Scott's Ivanhoe, 61 —contrary views, 62.

Hackett, James H., 119.
Hammond, 138.
Harby, Isaac, 75, note 82
Hardwicke, Lord. 159.
Harrison General, 135.
Hart Abraham, 70—Bernard, Emanuel B., 55, 56— Rev. Mr. 57.
Hartford, 91.
Hays, Jacob, 45, 146: note 49— Judah, 31; note 32-Moses, 81, 90; note 87—Solomon, 31, 164; note 32.

Hendricks, Benjamin, 54 —Harman 44.
Henricque, Jacob Cohen, 19, 23; note 16.
Henriquez, Isaac, freeman, 27; note 25—Isaac Nunez, 68; note 75—Shem, 68, note 75.
Henry III (act) 160.
Historical Society, German (of N. Y.) xii.—New York, xiv.—Jewish viii, ix, 8, 49, 54, 58, 62, 73; notes 4, 54. 58, 62, 66 and 67.
Holland, 2—deaf to Stuyvesant's anti Jewish prejudices, 9, 88, 91; note 5.
Hollander, J. H., on John Lumbrozo, 8, 62; notes 4, 66.
Hosack, Mr., note 120.
Hughes, John, note 120—Mrs. 145.
Hunter, Governor, petitioned by D'Lucena, 28.
Illan, Jan de, 9.
Independence, declaration of, 83, 118.
Indians descendants of lost tribes of Israel, 131, 137, 138.
Injustice, in New York colony, 51.
Inquisition, the xiii.
Intolerance of Spain, 2.
Introduction xi.
Ireland (author), 106.
Irving Washington, and Rebecca Gratz, 61.
Isaacs, 158—Abraham naturalized, 45; note 49—Isaac 78; note 84—Joseph 49; note 54—Rev. S.M. 57
Israel, David, held in N. Y. as pledge for payment, 23; note 7—Isaac, trade on Delaware 22, 154 note 18.
Italy, 88.
Ivanhoe 61.

Jackson, General, 91, 125, 132, 133, 134.
Jacob, Master, 151
Jacobs, Mr. 78; note 84—Joseph, 78 note 84.
Jacquet, vice-director 151.
Jamaica, 81, 85.
James, Duke of York (James II.) grants religious freedom, 26.

168   INDEX.

James I. (acts) 157.
Jameson, Dr. biography of Usselinx xv.
Janeway, William, 39, 40.
Jefferson, Thomas, president, 59, 63, 72, 118
Jeffrey Lord, 61
Jewish Historical Society, American, (its establishment) viii.
Jews*——their interest in the colonization of America,xi.--Spanish discovery of America, xii—as intermediaries between Moors and Christians, xii,—their scientific discoveries xii—spreading geographical science xiii, participation in Expeditions, xiii— secret Jews xiii, financiers aiding Columbus xiii, Jews in Mexico xiii, Jews as new Christians in Mexico, xiii,—in Brazil xvii,—liberty in Rhode Island, xiv,—in Netherland xv,—as share-holders of Dutch West India Co. xv, 9— attacked by Usselinx xvi,— as directors of the E & W. India Co, xvii, 9—in Brazil, promise aid xvii—desire naturalization xvii—disavow Christianity xvii— leaves Bahia for Amsterdam, xvii,—expelled from France, Spain and Portugal, 2—seeking refuge in Holland, and settle in Amsterdam, 4—in Holland, restricted socially but privileged ini politics 4,—antagonized by Catholics and Dutch Protestants 6— restrictions in ceremonial worship, 6, 13, note 11,—first settlement from Bahia 6—held in N. Y., for deficit in payment of passage money 7, 8, note 3,— Dutch government defends them against Stuyvesant,9 note 5—colony formed in Curacoa, 9—Jewish directors apply for special privileges of trade, 10—Stuyv. orders them out of N. Y. 11, note 10-tolerated in Rhode Island 13—settle there 14, 15—grant of land for cemetery in N. Y. 15— location 15-16—N. Y. Jews exempt from military service 16, 17; note 13—petitions for trading on Delaware River, 19 note 17— complain to friends in Holland, 21—trade at Fort Orange (Albany) 22, note 19—Jews admitted as citizens, 23—their incompetency as witnesses, 45, 46, notes, 53 and 54—not permitted to vote 46, 47. 51; notes 53, 54— prosperity of N. Y. colonists, 48, 49,50; note 5—in American Army 54; note 58—migrate to Philadelphia 55, 58, notes 58 and 62

Joghimsen, (Joachimsen?) Daniel, 32.
Johnson, Miss, 106, 123.
Jones, Col. Charles C., 67 note 73.
Jones, Judge Thomas, 164.
Juda, Baruch, 31, note 32.
Judah, Benjamin S., 139, 145, Emanuel, 103. Samuel B. H., dramatic writer, his career, 139.

Kalm, Swedish traveller, describes the customs and synagogal service of New York Jews, 48, 50 note 55.
Kayserling, Dr. Moses—on discov. of America,xii.—Portuguese discoveries xii—on Marranos, xiii— recent researches, xii—"Sephardim" xiii.
Keene, 109, 110.
Kent, Chancellor, 43—Nathan, Judge, 136.
King, Charles. 125, 126.
Kohler, Rev. Dr. xii.

La Cuya, (Lucena?) Abraham, taxed, 19, note 16.
Lamontagne, on Jewish trade, 21 note 17.
Lawrence. Eugene, on Jewish discoveries xiii,
Laying of the Corner Stone of N. Y. Hebrew Orphan Association v.
Lazarus, Michael, 76 note 82.

*Under this heading, only the principal events in early colonial history are summarized in chronological order.

Lee 59
Leesugg, Miss, 119.
Legal Status of the Jews 45, 49, 87, 89, 155, 161.
Legislature 63.
Leicester, 86.
Leira, the historical town of Estramadura flourished because of Jews, 4.
Levey, Richard, 22, 154, note 18.
Leisler, Governor, 26, 28.
Levy, Asser, protests against taxation 17, note 14—as champion, 18—as merchant in Albany 22; note 19—applies in vain for citizenship, 23, 32, 33—[Asser] Nathan, 31, 34, 43; note 32—Hayman, 52—his high standing, character and influence, 52-Isaac, 34—Moses, 34, 49; note 54—Zeporah, Miss, 54.
Lisbon, 29, 79, 80, 104; note 85.
Lockhart, 61.
London, 64, 69, 93, 108.
Longfellow, H. W. 81 note 85.
Lopez, Aaron, 76, 77, 78, 79, 82, 83, 85, 86, 89—Moses, 80, 89; note 85.
Louisiana, 75, 110, 116.
Lucena, Jacob, 22, note 19. See De Lucena.
Lumbrozo, Jacob, (John,) 8, 62; note 54, 66.
Lyon, Isaac Nathan, 78; note 84. See De Lyon.
Lyons, Rev. Jacques J., 57, 101.

Madison, President, 59, 72, 73—his indebtedness to Haym Salomon, 60, 63.
Marache, Solomon, 60.
Maranos,—secret Jews xiii—in Cuba, xiii, xvii.
Markens, Isaac, 87, 101; note 91.
Marques, Isaac Rodriguez 49; note 54.
Marvel, Andrew, on Amsterdam, 3.
Maryland, Jews in 8, 62, 64, 82—intolerance in, 63, 156.
Massachusetts, 91.
Maxwell, Hugh, 144.

Mears, Judah, 31, 34, note 32.
Medus, Simon, 82, note 88.
Mendez, Abraham, 26—Benjamin, 69—Solomon, 78; note 84.
Menasseh ben Israel to Cromwell, xvi.
Menorah, xii, xiii, 41; note 43.
Mercer 59.
Merritt, William, Mayor of N. Y., 39.
Mesa, Isaac, 23.
Meyer, Rev. Mr., 57.
Mexico—settlement in, xiii.
Mifflin, 59, 107.
Military service, exemption of Jews from 17; 54, 75, 16, note 13.
Miller, Rev. John, on location of first Synagogue, 27,
Minis, Abraham, Esther, Leah, 68, note 75; Philip, 70, Simeon, 68, 70, 73, note 75.
Mississippi 92, 93, 94.
Missouri, 92, 93, 94.
Molena, 68 note 75.
Monroe, James, 59, 109, 112, 116, 117, 124.
Moors, their scientific inventions, xii, 88.
Moranda, David, 68, note 75.
Moravians, 67.
Morris, George P. 122—Robert 59.
Moses, Isaac, Judah, Jacob, Moses 78; note 84.
Myers, Aaron, Benjamin, Moses, Naphtali, 78; note 84—Solomon 45, 78, notes 49, 84.

Napoleon, Louis (brother of Nap. I.) King of Holland, removes Jewish disabilities, 4.
Nathan Simon, 60.
Naturalization of Jews, 45, 49, 82, 155, 161 notes 49, 54.
New Bedford, 81 note 85.
New Castle 22.
New England xi, 75.
New Haven, 91.
New Orleans, 85, 90, 91, 116.
Newport, Jews settle in, 14, 15, 21, new arrivals, 29, 70, 76, 77, 79, 80, 82, 84 85, 86, 87, 89, 91, 92; notes 83, 84, 85.

New Netherland, see New York.
New York, Jews in xvii, 6, 58, 75.
Niagara River, 96, 128, note 92.
Noah, Manuel. 104—Mordecai M.
his career as statesman, politician, author, dramatist and journalist, his restoration schemes, 96, 102, 104; note 92—Shem, 68; note 75.
Norsemen, 91.
North Carolina 75, 156.
Nunez, 104, Dr. 31, 104; note 32—Joseph 31; note 32.
Nunis, Daniel, 68; note 75—Doctor 66, 67, 68: note 75—Moses, Mrs. N., Sipra, 68, note 75.

O'Callaghan, cited, 15.
Oglethorpe, General Geo., 64-established Jewish colony, 64—character, 66—eulogizes Jews, 66, 67—disobeys instructions injurious to Jews, 69, 70, 104.
Olivera, David, Isaac, Jacob, Leah, 68; note 75.
Orange, Fort, 13, 20, 21, 22.
Outrage upon a Jew by Oliver De Lancey, 51.

Pacheco, Benjamin Mendes, 31; note 32.
Packeckoe, Moses, 82.
Palestine, 91, 129.
Paris, 116.
Parliament, 64, 82, 83.
Payne John Howard, 120, 145.
Peixotto, Rev. Moses L. M., 56, 57.
Pennsylvania, Jews in, 58, 62, 75.
Philadelphia, 89, 99, 102, 103, 104, 105, 126. See Pennsylvania.
Phillips, Aaron J., 102, 103, 120—Jonas, 60—Jonas B., dramatist, his career, 145—Moses, S., 102.
Phillipse, Col. Frederick, 45.
Pimenta, Moses, 76. note 82.
Pinto, Rev. Jos. Isaac Jerushalem, 56.
Plymouth, xiv, 108.
Poland, 88.
Polock, Cushman, 72.
Portuguese, promise amnesty to Jews, xvii.
Preface, v.

Providence, 77, note 83.
Puff, Major Pindar, 141.
Puritans, xiv.

Quakers, objectionable, 14; in Newport, 77, note 83.

Raphall, Rabbi, 31, note 32.
Real, Vene, 68, note 75.
Restoration, schemes, of M. M. Noah, 127, 138.
Rhode Island, 77, 80, 82, 83, 84; note 83—Jews in xiv. 14, 21, 76.
Richmond, 99, settlement of Jews in, 101.
Riviera, Abraham, 31; note 32—Jacob, 70, 78, 79.
Robinson, Beverly, 68—W.D., 92, 94, 96.
Rodriguez, (Rodrigues), Isaac, 31, 45; notes 32, 49—J.R., 31, 78, 79; note 32.
Rogers, Robert, 162.
Romilly, Sir Samuel, 159.
Rosendale, Attorney General, 49, note 54.
Russell, Chas. R. Esq., 78, 86, note 84.
Rutgers, Harmanus, 38.

Sabbath, non-observance of, 11, 12; note 10.
Salem, 110.
Salomon, David, 78; note 84—Haym 58; staunch support of U.S. government, 58, 59; death 60; note 63.
Salvador, Francis, 65.
Savannah, settlement of Jews in, 64, 69, 70, 71, 72, 73, 74, 75, 76, 89, 91, 99, 103, 104.
Scott, Sir Walter, 61—his Jewish characters, 62.
Scovill, Jos. A. 42, 55, 56, 126, notes 46, 59.
Seixas, A.B. Judge, 131—Benjamin 55—Rev. Gershom, 56—Rev. Isaac, B, 57—Moses, 90.
Seward, William H. 47, 135, note 53.
Sharpe, Rev. John 29, note 30.
Shearith Israel, Cong., 33, 43, 44.

INDEX.

Sheftail Benjamin, 68, 70, 73, 74; note 75—Levy. [Levi] 69, 70, 72, 76; note 82—Mss. 67; note 73—Mordecai 68, 70, 74—Sheftail, 72, 74.
Simon, see De La Simon.
Simson, Joseph. 45, 70, note 49.
Sampson, 54, 70.
Skene, Mr. 61.
Sloughter, Governor, 27.
Smith, Ethan, 137, Goldwin, Professor on Jews, vi, historian, cited 48
Smollett, 157.
South Carolina—Jews in 70, 71, 75 note 82.
South River 13, 19, 20, 21, 22.
Southey, historian, cited xvii. 5.
Spanish settlements, xiii.
Sparks Jared, 54. note 58.
Spiller, 119.
Spinoza, 4.
St. Clair, 59.
Steuben, 59.
Stiles, Dr. 81, note 85.
Stone, Col. W. L. 143.
Straus, Hon Oscar S. 62, note 66.
Strictures on Jews by Rogers 162.
Stuyvesant on Jewish settlements xv.—his hostility, 8, 11—orders them from N. Y. 11, 17, note 10—censured 18; note 15—against Jewish trade, 20, 21; note 17—rebuked 21, 37, 42; note 46.
Suasso, Alvarez Lopez, 65.
Swanton, Robert, 44.
Synagogues described 27, 28, 30, 57, 58, 60. 71, 72, 73, 75, 80, 81, 85, 87, 90, 92, 95, 101, 108, note 85.

Taxation, unequal, 19.
Tennis, 39.
Thorburn, Grant, 32.
Thurlow, 158.

Tobias, Joseph, Michael, 76; note 82.
Tomlin's Dictionary, 157.
Touro, Abraham, D. 85, 90.—Rev. Isaac, 81, 85; note 87.—Jacob, 85, 90.—Judah, 90, 91.
Tripoli, 106, 107, 108.
Tuckerman, H. T., 80, note 85.
Tunis, 107, 108, 109, 110, 111, 113, 114, 121, 122, 130.

Usselinx, William, xv, his animosity toward Jews, xvi, xvii.
Utrecht, treaty of 3.

Van Buren, 133, 134, 135.
Van Halten Arent, 7, note 3.
Van Horne, Cornelius, 45.
Van Tienhoven, Cornelius 7, 11, 12; notes 3, 10.
Van Vinge 11, note 10.
Verbrugge, Johannes, 11, note 10
Verplanck Gulian C., 141.
Virginia 75, see Richmond.

Walworth, Chancellor, 44.
Washington, city, 116, 117,—Gen. George, 104
Webb, Colonel, 133, 134
Webbers, Wolfert, 37, 39.
Wheaton, Henry, 117, 118.
Wilkes, Miss, 61.
Willey, Noe, 39, 42—Roy, 39, 40, 41, 42
Webb, Col. 133.
Williams Roger, xiv, 13.
William the Silent, 3.
Wilson, 59.
Winterbotham, 71.
Wolcott, 140
Wolfertsen, Pieter, 7, note 3.
Wolf, Hon. Simon, 55, note 58. 60, note 63; pleads for Haym Salomon's descendants.

Young, Mrs. C. L. 106.

ERRATA.

Page 19, note, line 3. For "De Coster," read "Da Costa."
Page 26, line 23. For "may have it," read "may have had it."
Page 31, note, line 13. For "Riviero," read "Rivera."
Page 44, line 15. For "Harman," read "Harmon."
Page 45, lines 6, 11, 13, 16. For "Col. Phillips," read "Col. Phillipse."
Page 46, note, line 11. For "adapted," read "adopted."
Page 49, note, lines 3, 28. For "Brida," read "Breda."
Page 51, note, line 1. For "60," read "61."
Page 62, note, line 8. Word "Editor" omitted.
Page 75, note, line 10. For "natural," read "maternal."
Page 109, line 6. Substitute comma for period, "that" for "That."
Page 115, line 7. Substitute semi-colon for period, read "That" for "that."
Page 117, line 2. For "Presidency," read "President."
Page 135, line 18. For "after," read "afterwards."
Page 135, line 27. For "commercial," read "criminal."
Page 155, line 25. For "ever," read "every."

www.ingramcontent.com/pod-product-compliance
Lightning Source LLC
Chambersburg PA
CBHW020847160426
43192CB00007B/822